Fiber
Gathering

Fiber Gathering

Knit, Crochet, Spin and Dye more than 25 Projects
Inspired by America's Festivals

by Joanne Seiff

WILEY

Wiley Publishing, Inc.

Fiber Gathering: Knit, Crochet, Spin and Dye more than 25 Projects Inspired by America's Festivals

Published by Wiley Publishing, Inc., Hoboken, New Jersey

For general information on our other products and services or to obtain technical support please contact our Customer Care Department within the U.S. at (800) 762-2974, outside the U.S. at (317) 572-3993 or fax (317) 572-4002.

Wiley also publishes its books in a variety of electronic formats. Some content that appears in print may not be available in electronic books. For more information about Wiley products, please visit our web site at www.wiley.com.

Library of Congress Cataloging-in-Publication Data:
Seiff, Joanne, 1973-
  Fiber gathering : knit, crochet, spin and dye more than 25 projects inspired by America's festivals / by Joanne Seiff.
    p. cm. 41935486   10/09
  ISBN-13: 978-0-470-28935-8
  ISBN-10: 0-470-28935-X
1. Textile crafts. 2. Craft festivals. I. Title.
 TT699.S42 2009
 746—dc22
                        2008046703

Printed in China

10 9 8 7 6 5 4 3 2 1

Book production by Wiley Publishing, Inc., Composition Services

Credits

Acquisitions Editor
Roxane Cerda

Project Editor
Suzanne Snyder

Editorial Manager
Christina Stambaugh

Publisher
Cindy Kitchel

Vice President and Executive Publisher
Kathy Nebenhaus

Interior Design
Elizabeth Brooks

Cover Design
José Almaguer

Photography
Jeff Marcus

About the Author

Joanne Seiff enjoys making things from scratch; her mother taught her to knit when she was five and she learned to spin at 12. Her spinning wheel and knitting needles accompanied her to college and beyond. Joanne earned her undergraduate degree in Comparative Literature and Near Eastern Studies from Cornell University. She holds a Master's degree in Education from the George Washington University and a Master's degree in Religious Studies from the University of North Carolina at Chapel Hill.

Joanne is a writer, knitwear designer and educator. Her fiction and non-fiction writing appears in a variety of print and online publications, with a focus on fiber arts, food, the environment, and religious issues. Her fiber art and handspun have been featured in several galleries, including ones in New York City and Berea, Kentucky. She's proud to be the recipient of a Kentucky Foundation for Women grant and the Kentucky Art Council's 2007 Al Smith Individual Artist Fellowship for her non-fiction.

Joanne has taught summer camp, religious school, high school, college, workshops and adult education courses. Her pupils range from four year olds to adults. She loves to learn and explore, whatever the topic: spinning, knitting, writing, music, religious studies or cooking. Her past fiber arts experience includes teaching introductory hand spinning classes at Duke University, as well as teaching about textile traditions on the frontier at the Kentucky Museum. She's even taught a cooking workshop on boiling spaghetti for Duke undergraduates!

When she's not spinning, knitting or cooking, Joanne often spends time outdoors with her absent-minded biology professor husband, Jeff. Dr. Jeff Marcus studies butterfly genetics when he's not shooting photos of sheep for her books and articles. Gardening and reading are some of her other pleasures, along with walking her bird dogs, Harry and Sally. (Harry is a setter mix, and Harry's pet, Sally, is a pointer mix.)

Read her work or see more of her designs at her Web site, www.joanneseiff.com and follow her daily adventures on her blog, Yarn Spinner, at www.joanneseiff.blogspot.com.

Acknowledgments

An undertaking like this one requires lots of help, and for that, I am indebted. Many thanks to the designers who contributed to this book; creativity lends so much to our enjoyment of every festival. Also, all thanks to my models, who are regular (beautiful) folk who smiled for everyone to see: Tim Shehan, Bonnie Reed and Truman Reed, Jessica Dunnegan, Bridget Sutton, Remy Attig, Tia Hughes and Laura Sinise. For suggestions, support, contacts and clever ideas, I am grateful to, in no particular order: Gregory Kompes, Deb Robson, Deborah Balmuth, Linda Roghaar, Melanie Falick, Cat Bordhi, Shannon Okey, Ilana Marcus and the many other luminaries who offered me advice. Thank you to Kate Nachman's parents, for putting us up on short notice in New Hampshire and to my family and my husband's, who put us up in Virginia and New York, visited with us at festivals and supported us along the way. Harry and Sally, the dogs, wish to thank Rachel Barber, dog sitter extraordinaire, as well as Greystone Animal Hospital and Dogs Day Out for taking good care of us while our owners cavorted with sheep and llamas. (Thanks for giving us our duck and potato kibble!)

I was the lucky recipient of the 2007 Kentucky Arts Council's Al Smith Individual Artist Fellowship, funded by both the Commonwealth of Kentucky and the National Endowment of the Arts. This financial support kept me eating and travelling to festivals—*a great nation deserves great art*, and great art includes spinning and knitting! Please consult the resource guide to support all the businesses who donated their yarn and other wares. Thank you to all these kind companies who contributed to make these rich designs possible.

It was my great good fortune to work with Roxane Cerda, my editor at Wiley, and with Suzanne Snyder; thank you is hardly enough for the support I've received from my publisher. Donna Druchunas, my faithful tech editor, deserves a medal for her patience and attention to detail! Many wonderful people smiled at us and offered valuable information at every festival; these countless exchanges made this book's research a delight. Finally, to my husband, Jeffrey Marcus, who supported and enabled me to make this adventure possible, many thanks. My professor was such a great travel companion…going to twelve (or more?) events in 2007 and encouraging me to buy all that yarn and those extra fleeces, just in case I might need it later. Jeff burned the candle at both ends to fulfill his obligations as both a biology professor AND to take all the photos for this book. Wonder why all those animal photos have so much personality? It helps to have a professional along—maybe his Ph.D. in Zoology helped!

Table of Contents

Northeast

South

Midwest

West

Introduction

Throughout history, we've gathered together in the market square. We're there to buy and sell, to get good deals on fibers, fabrics, fruits, vegetables, and bread, but we're also there to see friends, gossip, trade recipes, and admire new clothes. We've got an eye on each other's animals, and we're going to keep them from getting into any trouble. It's our chance to hold someone else's baby or to congratulate a new grandmother. It's a chance to connect, to touch, and to bond with others.

These days, it's easy to feel like we live in scary times, and sometimes we're less neighborly than we used to be. Our lives are filled with long distances and technology. We're more likely to make cyberfriends than visit with someone down the street. Our lives are full of work, school, and caretaking, but how many of us still live near our families? Our hometowns? How do we reach out to one another?

In the United States, the growth of interest in fiber arts such as knitting, spinning, weaving, hand-dyeing, and needlework, and in the institution of the fiber festival itself, has been astonishing. While there are huge long-standing events such as the Maryland Sheep and Wool Festival with 50,000 attendees, there are just as many new festivals and small gatherings that crop up every year. The rise of the stitch 'n' bitch session, the knitting blog world, and the many crafty online groups barely meet this need to gather. In a world full of mass-produced textiles, many women (and some men) are reaching out to one another, and reaching back to a slower, more careful way of creating clothing, art, and meaning. We're doing this by meeting, buying, learning, and teaching at fiber festivals.

To write this book, I travelled to fairgrounds and events across the country. At each festival, I found something special, something I couldn't resist purchasing, touching, and discussing with a farmer or friend. I always met warm, kind people who rushed to embrace this idea of festival as much more than just buying and selling. It was a time to learn, to visit, to celebrate new ideas, and to reunite with old friends.

In every setting, I met people who enthusiastically embraced me and my thoughts about festivals, and eagerly awaited this book's publication. Many talented designers stepped up and asked to be included in this book. They couldn't wait to offer their creativity to honor their favorite festivals, fiber arts, and yarns. Since each festival contains myriad fiber supplies, skills, and activities, I've interspersed these amazing designs throughout the book to fit each chapter's focus, but many of these designers and teachers are known (and welcomed!) throughout the entire festival circuit. I hope you'll find their project concepts relevant no matter which festival is your personal favorite.

Use the patterns to fit with your festival experiences. Please substitute your special festival finds for the yarns and materials in each design to fit your preferences, or if you prefer, follow the designer's original inspiration by using the Resources section in the back of the book to find what you need to create your own masterpiece and bring those festival memories alive at home.

At each event, I was overwhelmed with excited people who asked to be notified when the book came out. Folks, here it is! Bring to it all your own festival experiences and adventures, and be open to hearing about the outstanding diversity of this age-old, nationwide phenomenon. Welcome to the 21st-century marketplace. Let's meet, greet, eat lamb treats and other fair delicacies, visit the animals, fondle their fiber, and enjoy it together— at our own Fiber Gatherings—everywhere.

West

Northeast

1. Maryland Sheep & Wool
2. Rhinebeck, New York State Sheep and Wool Festival
3. New Hampshire Sheep and Wool Festival

South

4. Southeastern Animal Fiber Fair, North Carolina
5. The Tennessee State Fair

Midwest

6. Michigan Fiber Festival
7. Missouri—Heart of America Sheep Show and Fiber Fest
8. Sheep Shearing Event, Kentucky

Northeast

chapter 1

Maryland Sheep and Wool Festival

N ewcomers to Maryland Sheep and Wool, held the first full weekend in May at the Howard County Fairgrounds, often say that they encounter sensory overload. Crowds of festival goers surge up the path from a nearby grassy field, covered with thousands of cars. Music fills the air as an Old Time band tunes up. Eager shoppers consider the purchase of dye plants, yarn, fleeces, and sheep pens within feet of the festival's entrance. The air is filled with pungent odors of barbequed lamb, fresh smelling spring air, and more subtle smells of hay, animals, and freshly shorn fleece.

This is the first festival I ever attended, and my "home" festival. For perhaps 15 years I've seen the festival grow and change. Today, one hears that this festival, in its 34th year, has upwards of 50,000 visitors in one day, and I'd believe it.

People come to festivals for various reasons. Sometimes, I've had a shopping list and left with a spinning wheel or a special fleece. My mother often purchases several sweaters' worth of knitting yarn, and my friends leave with looms, books, cheese, frozen lamb, and other treasures. In lean years I've spent the festival differently, visiting with friends, trying out new spinning wheels, and enjoying the enormity of the event. I'd eat a lamb gyro or burger, watch sheep breed competitions and sheep dog demonstrations, and collect inexpensive mementos, ideas, and connections to cherish throughout the year.

Although special things are available at all festivals, the enormity of Maryland Sheep & Wool and its many vendors allow people to focus on purchasing exactly what they want—no matter what it is. In recent years, the festival has become known for its hand-dyed and hand-painted yarns and roving. Wool, cashmere, alpaca, rayon, Tencel, superwash or hemp, laceweight, sock yarn or bulky, whatever your preferences, you can find it here.

Knitters, spinners, and weavers all have their strategies. Some fiber-crazy folks make a beeline to see Brooks Farm's special hand-dyed yarns; others race to find Hatchtown spindles, Socks That Rock yarn, or to get a deal on a special spinning wheel. Along the way, everyone (it seems) bumps into someone they know. Even if you don't see friendly faces, you might see someone wearing a sweater that matches the design you knitted last year. This is a chance for fiber artists from up and down the east coast to be around people and interests they love.

As a result of this huge event and shopping opportunity, many fly into a nearby airport to attend. At Baltimore-Washington International Airport, you can recognize the other festival goers by their huge carry-ons, bursting with wool, and their t-shirts, bags, and other festival paraphernalia. Festival goers even greet complete strangers, showing off great finds with one another while waiting for their planes to board.

Those who buy raw fleeces but are traveling long distances home by plane or in a car already crowded with purchases have easy solutions available. One can buy the fleeces and drop them off at one of the many fiber processors. These folks fill trailers full of fleece and drive home to their mills. After washing, picking, and carding fleeces into lofty, fluffy roving for spinning, they will ship everything right to the purchaser's home.

Sheep farmers from all over the country bring their animals here to compete for awards. The pens are filled with a buzz—not just of activity, but of the trimming shears. Some breeds of sheep are given a trim so judges can evaluate their meat market potential, while others pant in full fleece, to be judged on the basis of their fiber.

These top competitions help shepherds nationwide to evaluate the quality of their livestock. Young 4-H farmers learn the ropes and often sleep near their animals. Other family members network, making connections that may one day boost their flocks through the purchase of a prize ram. Near the pens, fleeces wait for savvy spinners, who shop by meeting the shepherds and the sheep before purchasing their fiber.

Other shepherds participate in the festival's livestock shows simply by putting their animals on display. Maryland Sheep and Wool has an extensive display of rare sheep breeds each year, with live examples. If sheep aren't your thing, you can visit llamas, alpacas, and angora rabbits as well. This is a chance to see a diverse and very competitive array of fiber on the hoof.

Shearer Emily Chamelin

This festival offers it all: classes, competitions, and free demonstrations and performances for those who aren't shopping. Maryland Sheep and Wool Festival is a good reflection of its fast paced, east coast hustle and bustle location. The entrance may be traffic-clogged and the crowds can be overwhelming for those who don't expect it. Vendors fight hard to land booths at this festival and say that selling their wares here is always good for business.

On years when I've flown back to see my parents and go to this festival, I've actually had to remove things from my suitcase on the way back so it was light enough to be checked. As I hauled books, knitting projects, and other goodies in my carry-on bag through the airport, I remembered why each purchase was worthwhile . . . and absolutely necessary!

The Food

Walk down the fairway at the Howard County Fairgrounds, and prepare for a lamb feast. Although choices have improved for vegetarians in recent years, the main dish on the menu here is L-A-M-B. Pit Lamb sandwich, sausage, ribs, shish kabob, gyros, lamb burgers, lamb stew in a bread bowl—if it can be done with lamb and eaten while strolling the fair, it's served at this festival. Also popular are the numerous fresh lemonade stands, funnel cake, ice cream, éclair, caramel corn, nuts, homemade soda pop, potato chip ribbons, and other fair delights. While you may come to the fair to shop, you'll surely be sidetracked by the food. Groups of friends share tastes, and in one rare instance, a lady who didn't know us walked right up and said, "You've got to try this funnel cake! Here's mine—and don't worry, I haven't got any communicable diseases!" (Yes, spinners and knitters are this friendly!)

Sheep Dog Demonstrations

On many farms, the sheep dog, often a border collie, is indispensable. Bred with a unique combination of herding instincts and brains, this dog can round up hundreds of sheep on the farm. The farmer, (also called a handler), uses a special combination of whistle calls and voice commands to help his or her dog to do quickly the job that would take one farmer all day. Sheep can be moved from pasture to barn or from field to field without any trauma. How? Through the careful crouch, sharp stare (called "the eye") and herding skills of a dog who looks like a predator to a sheep. Sheep automatically respond to these dogs' crouches and stares, by edging away. It's in their genes to "escape" from a predator.

At Maryland Sheep and Wool, these hardworking farm dogs with names like Scout or Aggie are taken off the farm and brought to demonstrate their skills to crowds of 200 or more. Three times a day, these dogs show the crowds what they can do. Since bringing a flock of sheep to a gravel pen at the festival isn't practical, the demonstration flock consists of no more than 10 hair sheep, (varieties that don't grow wool) who can take the stress of being herded round and round for the festival goers' education. In order to simulate the farm, competitive dog trials all over the world use picket fences, pens, and cones to challenge the dogs. The smartest dogs have such focus that they are unaffected by crowds. They listen carefully to the handler's commands and the sheep move en masse in complicated figure-eight patterns, in and around "bridges," Y gates, and into and out of a pen in the middle of the ring. The crowds cheer for the dogs, but the dogs have eyes only for the sheep—and their handlers.

At the end of their runs, panting with excitement and exertion, the dogs must be leashed or hooked with a shepherd's crook to keep them from taking off again, to work more. This drive to work has to be monitored; dog handlers in hot climates have a special command to prevent heat exhaustion. That command forces the dog to jump into water to cool down so that their sheep herding obsession doesn't become deadly. In the demonstration ring at the festival, the applause makes the owners and handlers proud to show the city slickers their best working farm "tool." The dogs can't wait to get back to their home ground, the farm, to herd and work again.

Mary Jane Socks

These toe-up socks with a short row heel provide fun nostalgia and a funky picot ruffle for those of us who love their Mary Jane shoes. This pattern is ideal for using every last bit of precious hand-dyed yarns. While the Mary Jane socks are designed with a round toe and short row heel, an experienced sock knitter should be able to substitute whatever heel and toe suit the wearer best.

Skill level

Intermediate

Size

Women's Medium (Large)

Finished Measurements

Foot circumference: 8 (9)" (20.5 [23]cm)

Length from toe to heel: 9 (9½)" (23 [24]cm)

Materials

- 350 yd. (320m) of any superfine weight or fingering weight yarn that knits up at the appropriate gauge

Sample knit with: The Barefoot Spinner *Superwash Fingering Weight Hand-Dyed Sock Yarn* (100 percent superwash wool; 350 yd. [320m] per 3 oz. [85g] skein): 1 skein; color Rose

- Set of 4 size 2 (2.75mm) double-pointed needles *or size needed to obtain gauge*
- Stitch marker
- Tapestry needle

Gauge

30 sts and 41 rnds = 4" (10cm) in St st

Special Stitch

Backward Yarn-Over: With purl side facing, bring yarn to the back under needle, and then over the top. (The leading side of the loop will be on the back of the needle.) For more information about this technique, see *Simple*

Socks: Plain and Fancy (Nomad Press, 2004) by Priscilla Gibson-Roberts.

Instructions

Note When only one set of numbers is listed, it is applicable for both sizes.

Toe

Using 1 dpn, cast on 6 sts.

Preparation row: Kf&b across—12 sts.

Distribute sts evenly onto 3 needles. Join and place marker, being careful not to twist sts.

Rnd 1: *K1, kf&b; rep from * to end of rnd—18 sts.

Rnd 2: *K2, kf&b; rep from * to end of rnd—24 sts.

Continue in this way, evenly inc 6 sts in each rnd, another 6 (7) times—60 (66) sts, 20 (22) sts on each needle.

Work even in St st (knit every rnd) until foot measures 7 (7½)" (18 [19]cm) or desired length.

Heel

Beg at marker, distribute sts as follows: 15 (16) sts on first needle (#1), 30 (34) sts on second needle (#2), and 15 (16) sts on third needle (#3).

Work the heel over 30 (32) sts, back and forth on needles #1 and #3 as follows:

Row 1 (RS): On needle #1, k14 (15).

Row 2 (WS): Turn work, backward YO, p28 (30), continuing across to needle #3.

Next row (RS): Turn work, YO, k10 (12), k2tog-tbl, (YO and next st on needle), closing the gap.

Next row (WS): Turn work, backward YO, p11 (13), p2tog (YO and next st on needle), closing the gap.

Next row (RS): Turn work, YO, k until reaching 2 YOs, k3tog-tbl, (2 YOs and next st on needle).

Next row (WS): Turn work, backward YO, p until reaching 2 YOs, p3tog, (2 YOs and next st on needle).

Repeat the last 2 rows, continuing to turn work and decrease until all YO pairs have been worked. At the end of the last p row, p3tog (2 YOs and the last st on the needle).

Next row (RS): Turn work, YO, k30 (34), k2tog (YO and first st on needle #2); knit across to the last st on needle #2; k2tog (last st on needle #2 and the YO on needle #3); knit rem 15 (16) sts on needle #3.

Cuff

Return to knitting in the round.

Work 2" (5cm) in St st.

Next rnd: *K1, p1; rep from * to end of rnd.

Continue working k1, p1 ribbing for 4" (10cm) or until cuff is desired length.

Row 3 (RS): Turn work, YO, k27 (29).

Row 4 (WS): Turn work, backward YO, p until first paired sts made with a st with YO attached—26 (28) sts purled.

Row 5 (RS): Turn work, YO, k until first paired sts made with YO attached—25 (27) sts knitted.

Repeat rows 4 and 5, with fewer sts worked in St st each time, until 10 (12) sts rem between the YOs and you have just completed the following WS row: backward YO, p10 (12) sts.

Picot Ruffle

Bind off 2 sts. *Sl 1 st back to left-hand needle. Using the single cast-on (also called backward loop cast-on, see p. 152), cast on 3 sts, then bind off 5 sts. Rep from * until all sts have been bound off.

Finishing

Using tapestry needle, weave in ends, making sure to connect the first picot ruffle to the last one on the cuff. Close toe tip with a running stitch as a drawstring to create a smooth inside seam. Make second sock for best results!

Spirited Entrelac Polo

I love using hand-painted yarns, and one of my favorite producers is Jennifer of Spirit Trail Fiberworks. Spirit Trail sock yarn is always a sellout at fiber festivals, but the merino/silk I've used here is my favorite of the company's yarns because of the lovely way that the fibers take the dye, and also because it feels so good while knitting and wearing. This design popped into my head at a spring sheep and wool festival, and I jotted down a sketch as soon as I got home. It uses entrelac patterning to show off the subtle colors in the yarn, but puts the shaping and sizing in the side panels rather than in the entrelac. It would also work well in cotton, because the stitch pattern and the horizontally knit sides and sleeves will minimize cotton's tendency to "grow."

Designed by Shelia January

Skill level
Intermediate

Size
S (M, L, XL)

Finished Measurements
Bust: 36 (40½, 42½, 46)" (91.5 [102.9, 108, 116.8] cm)

Materials
- 1,040 (1,150, 1,240, 1,420) yd. (951 [1,052, 1,134, 1,298]m) of any medium weight or worsted weight yarn that knits up at the appropriate gauge

Sample knit with: Spirit Trail Fiberworks *Minerva* (50 percent merino wool, 50 percent silk; 400 yd. [366m] per 5.7 oz. [161g] skein), colorway Antique Tapestry, 3 (3, 4, 4) skeins

- US size 7 (4.5mm) circular needle 24" (61cm) long, *or size to obtain gauge*
- US size 7 (4.5mm) circular needle, 16" (41cm) long
- US size 6 (4mm) needles, straight needles or circular needle at least 24" (61cm) long
- Set of 4 US size 6 (4mm) double point needles, at least 6" (15cm) long
- Stitch markers
- Stitch holders
- Tapestry needle

Gauge
18 sts and 24 rows = 4" (10cm) over St st using US size 7 (4.5mm) needles

Stitch Patterns
Entrelac Pattern
Foundation Row Triangles
Beg with RS facing.

Row 1 (RS): K2tog, turn.

Row 2: P1, turn.

Row 3: K2, turn.

Row 4: P2, turn.

Row 5: K3, turn.

Row 6: P3, turn.

Row 7: K4, turn.

Row 8: P4, turn.

Row 9: K5, turn.

Row 10: P5, turn.

Row 11: K6, turn.

Row 12: P6, turn.

Row 13: K6 (on ninth triangle only, k5, k2tog instead), do not turn *except* on the ninth triangle.

Tier 1 Triangles and Rectangles

Beg with WS facing.

Right Side Triangle:

Worked once at beg of tier.

Row 1 (WS): P1, turn.

Row 2: K1, turn.

Row 3: P2, turn.

Row 4: K2, turn.

Row 5: Pf&b, p2tog, turn.

Row 6: K3, turn.

Row 7: Pf&b, p1, p2tog, turn.

Row 8: K4, turn.

Row 9: Pf&b, p2, p2tog, turn.

Row 10: K5, turn.

Row 11: Pf&b, p3, p2tog, do not turn.

Purl Rectangle:

Repeat 8 times across tier.

Row 1 (WS): Pick up and purl 6 sts from the edge of the previous row rectangle. Slip the last picked-up st to the left needle, p2tog, turn.

Row 2 (and all RS rows): K6, turn.

Rows 3, 5, 7, and 9: Sl1 pw, p4, p2tog, turn.

Row 11: Sl1 pw, p4, p2tog, do not turn.

Left Side Triangle:

Worked once at end of tier.

Row 1 (WS): Pick up and purl 6 sts, turn.

Row 2: K6, turn.

Row 3: Sl1 pw, p3, p2tog, turn.

Row 4: K5, turn.

Row 5: Sl1 pw, p2, p2tog, turn.

Row 6: K4, turn.

Row 7: Sl1 pw, p1, p2tog.

Row 8: K3, turn.

Row 9: Sl1 pw, p2tog.

Row 10: K2, turn.

Row 11: P2tog. Keeping the last st on the needle, turn work to begin Tier 2. This last st will replace the first picked-up st on the first knit rectangle.

Tier 2 Knit Rectangles

Begin with RS facing. Repeat 9 times across tier.

Row 1: Pick up and knit 6 sts from the edge of the previous row rectangle or triangle. (On the first rectangle the last remaining st from the previous tier will replace the first st to be picked up) Slip the last picked-up st to the left needle and ssk with the next st. Turn.

Row 2 (and all WS rows): P6, turn.

Rows 3, 5, 7, and 9: Sl1 kw, k4, ssk, turn.

Row 11: Sl1 kw, k4, ssk, do not turn *except* on the ninth rectangle at the end of the tier.

End Row Triangles

Begin with RS facing and after completing Tier 1.

Row 1: Pick up 6 sts, slipping last picked-up st to the left needle, ssk with the slipped st and the next st, turn. (On all succeeding triangles, you will have 1 st on the needle and will only be picking up 5 sts.)

Row 2: P6, turn.

Row 3: Ssk, k3, ssk, turn.

Row 4: P5, turn.

Row 5: Ssk, k2, ssk, turn

Row 6: P4, turn.

Row 7: Ssk, k1, ssk, turn

Row 8: P3, turn.

Row 9: Ssk twice, turn.

Row 10: P2, turn.

Row 11: Sl1, k2tog, psso, keeping the resulting last st on the right needle to become the first st of the next triangle.

On last triangle, break yarn and pull end through the last st.

Double Knit Edge Pattern

Worked over first and last 5 sts of the side panels. Slip all sts knitwise.

Row 1 (RS): K1, sl1 wyif, k1, sl1 wyif, k1.

Row 2 (WS): Sl1 wyib, p1, sl1 wyib, p1, sl1 wyib.

Rep rows 1 and 2 for patt.

Instructions

Note *Due to the building block nature of entrelac and the way that the decreases are constructed for the neck opening, all sizes of the sweater are the same length. As it is designed, the sweater will fall at the hip for a small, and just below the waist for an extra large. If a different length is desired, the sweater can be lengthened or shortened by the depth of a combination of one Tier 1 row and one Tier 2 row. This means that the length will probably be changed by at least 1½ –2" (3.8–5.1cm). Remember, if you lengthen the Front and Back panels, you'll need to increase the number of stitches picked up on the sides by the appropriate amount and you may need extra yarn.*

Back Entrelac Panel

With size 6 or smaller 24" circular needles, cast on 64 sts and work 1" (2.5cm) in garter stitch (knit all rows).

On next row, work 9 Foundation Row Triangles across the garter stitch hem—54 sts rem, 6 sts in each triangle. The triangles will be angled on the cable of the needle.

Work, alternating between Tier 1 and Tier 2 patterns, until the Back measures approximately 19¼" (48.9cm). End after completing a Tier 1 row.

Next entrelac row: Work 3 Tier 2 Knit Rectangles, then work 3 End Row Triangles, resulting in 24 bound off sts. Keep the last st from the bound-off triangles to begin working 3 more Tier 2 Knit Rectangles. You will still have the first 3 rectangles worked on the right needle (18 sts). Do not work these sts for the next 2 entrelac rows.

Left Shoulder

Entrelac row 1 (WS): Work Tier 1 for the first Left Side Triangle and 2 Purl Rectangles, turn. (Do not work the Right Side Triangle.)

Back Entrelac Panel

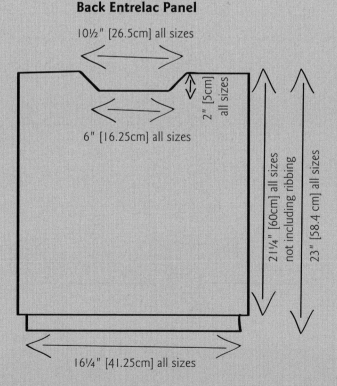

10½" [26.5cm] all sizes

6" [16.25cm] all sizes

2" [5cm] all sizes

21¼" [60cm] all sizes not including ribbing

23" [58.4 cm] all sizes

16¼" [41.25cm] all sizes

Entrelac Back Panel Shaping

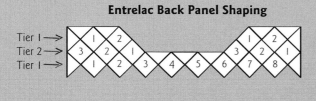

Tier 1 →
Tier 2 →
Tier 1 →

Repeat Tier 1 and Tier 2 to Shoulder Shaping

Tier 2 →
Tier 1 →
Foundation →
Triangles

Entrelac row 2 (RS): Bind off 5 sts, then use the last st to replace the first pick-up st of the first End Row Triangle. Work 2 End Row Triangles. Break yarn and pull through last rem st.

Right Shoulder

Turn work, and attach the yarn to the neck edge to begin working the reserved 18 sts.

Entrelac row 1 (WS): Do not work the Tier 1 Right Side Triangle, bind off 5 sts, then use the last st to replace the first pick-up st of the following 2 Tier 1 Purl Rectangles. Work 1 Tier 1 Left Side Triangle, turn.

Entrelac row 2 (RS): Work 2 End Row Triangles. Break yarn and pull through last rem st.

Front Entrelac Panel

Work as for Back until piece measures approximate 16½" (41.9cm) including the hem. End after completing a WS row (Tier 1).

Note If the neck shaping is begun on a WS row (Tier 1), the neckline will not be symmetrical.

Right Shoulder and Neck Shaping

Entrelac row 1 (RS): Begin a Tier 2 row, and work 4 Knit Rectangles, turn. (The rest of the work can be put on a stitch holder at this point.)

Entrelac row 2 (WS): Bind off 5 sts, work 3 Tier 1 Purl Rectangles. On the first rectangle only, do not slip the first st of the purl rows, purl these sts instead. Finish the row with a Tier 1 Right Side Triangle.

Entrelac row 3: Work Tier 2, making 3 Knit Triangles only, turn.

Front Entrelac Panel

10½" [26.5cm] all sizes

21¼" [60cm] all sizes not including ribbing

23" [58.4 cm] all sizes

16¼" [41.25cm] all sizes

Entrelac Front Panel Shaping

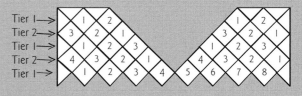

Tier 1 →
Tier 2 →
Tier 1 →
Tier 2 →
Tier 1 →

Repeat Tier 1 and Tier 2 to Shoulder Shaping

Tier 2 →
Tier 1 →
Foundation →
Triangles

Entrelac row 4: Work Tier 1 as follows. Bind off 5 sts, using the sixth st as the first st of the next rectangle, work 2 Purl Rectangles and 1 Left Side Triangle, turn.

Entrelac row 5: Work 2 End Row Triangles. Break yarn and pull through last rem st.

Left Shoulder and Neck Shaping

Entrelac row 1 (RS): Put the sts that have been on a holder back on the needle, and working from the RS, attach the yarn in the middle of the neck (the point of the V). Bind off 5 sts. Use the sixth st of the first group as the first picked-up st of the next rectangle, and work the 4 rectangles remaining in the row as Tier 2 Knit Rectangles, turn.

Entrelac row 2 (WS): Work a Tier 1 Left Side Triangle and 3 Tier 1 Purl Rectangles. Do not finish the row with a Right Side Triangle, instead, turn the work.

Entrelac row 3: Bind off 5 sts. Use the sixth st of the first group as the first picked-up st of the next rectangle, and work the 3 rectangles remaining in the row as Tier 2 Knit Rectangles, turn.

Entrelac row 4: Work a Tier 1 Left Side Triangle and 2 Tier 1 Purl Rectangles. Do not finish the row with a Right Side Triangle, instead, turn the work.

Entrelac row 5: Bind off 5 sts in knit. Use the sixth st of the first group as the first picked-up st of an End Row Triangle. Work a second End Row Triangle. Break yarn and pull through last rem st.

Sew shoulder seams, matching the entrelac pattern. It is very helpful to block the joined Front and Back entrelac panels before continuing.

Sides and Sleeves (make 2)

Using the size 7 or larger 24" (61cm) circular needle, and working from the RS bottom edge of the Front Entrelac Panel, pick up and knit 106 sts on each side of the shoulder seam—212 sts total.

Note An easy way to pick up the sts is to pick up 6 sts in the bottom garter borders, then an equal amount of stitches in each of the triangle sections up the sides of the Front and Back panels. For example, if there are 10 triangles on the sides of each of the entrelac panels, 6 stitches would be picked up in the garter stitch border of the Front panel, 10 in each of the side triangles of the Front, and over the shoulder seam, 10 in each of the side triangles of the Back panel, and 6 in the back bottom garter stitch border for a total of 212.

Setup row: Work first 5 sts in Edge Pattern, place marker (pm), work in St st (knit RS rows, purl WS rows) to last 5 sts, pm, work last 5 sts in Edge Pattern.

Work in St st and Edge Pattern as est until the side measures 1½ (1¾, 2, 2½)" (3.8 [4.5, 5.1, 6.4]cm) from the picked-up sts.

Join the first and last 54 (51, 48, 44) sts of the side with the three-needle bind-off (see p. 155). The center 104 (110, 116, 124) sts rem on the needle.

Underarm Shaping

Continue working back and forth in St st and work 24 rows, dec 1 st at the beg of each row. When 24 sts have been bound off (12 at each side of the work), join the rem 80 (86, 92, 100) sts on the 16" (41cm) circular needle and work the sleeves in the round as follows:

Sleeve

Join work, placing marker at the beginning (underarm seam) of the sleeve.

Knit 4 rnds.

Begin sleeve shaping: Continue working in st st (knit every rnd) and at the same time dec 1 st on each side of the marker every other row 1 (1, 2, 3) times, then every fourth row until 48 (50, 52, 56) sts rem.

Note Use an ssk dec to the left of the marker, and a k2tog to the right of the marker.

If necessary, work even until piece measures 18 (19, 19, 20)" (45.7 [48.3, 48.3, 50.8]cm) from the picked up sts. On the last round, dec 6 sts evenly around the arm—42 (44, 46, 50) sts rem.

Change to dpns for cuff.

Work in garter stitch (purl 1 rnd, knit 1 rnd) for 1" (2.5cm), beginning with a purl round.

Bind off.

Rep on the opposite side for the second Side and Sleeve.

Finishing

Collar

Using size 6 or smaller 16" (41cm) circular needle, with RS facing and beg at the V of the Front Entrelac Panel, pick up 34 sts from right neck edge, pick up 51 sts from back neck edge, and pick up 34 sts from left neck edge—119 sts total.

Turn and work back and forth as follows:

Row 1 (RS): *K1, p1; rep from * to last st, k1.

Row 2 (WS): *P1, k1; rep from * to last st, p1.

Work another 4 rows of k1, p1 ribbing. Switch to size 7 or larger 16" (41cm) circular needle.

Continue in k1, p1 ribbing until the collar measures 3¼" (8.3cm) from the beg of the ribbing. Bind off in knit if working from RS, and in purl if working from WS.

Sew underarm gusset seams. Weave in ends. When weaving in the yarn end at the V of the neckline, use this opportunity to tighten up the V, both to neaten and to reinforce at this point.

Wash and lay flat to block, paying special attention to the side seams. They will need to be flattened because of the three-needle bind-off. Fold the collar down to dry.

Designer Bio

Shelia January is a longtime knitter and designer who lives on a farm in Oregon. Shelia, who worked for 28 years in the financial services industry, says knitting keeps her sane. She became a spinner just a few years ago and now collects spinning wheels as well as yarn. She knits and designs with her homespun yarn as well as commercial yarns, and has taught spinning and knitting at retreats and shops in New York, Massachusetts, and Virginia. Shelia attends lots of fiber festivals, too. You can visit her blog at www.letstalkstash.blogspot.com.

Sleeve/Side Unit

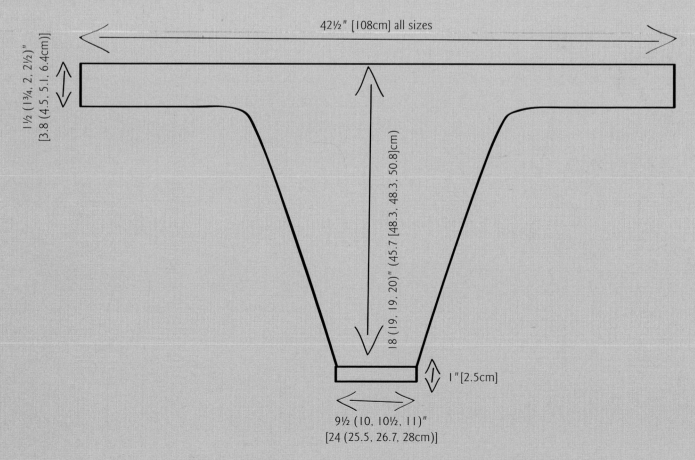

42½" [108cm] all sizes

1½ (1¾, 2, 2½)" [3.8 (4.5, 5.1, 6.4cm)]

18 (19, 19, 20)" (45.7 (48.3, 48.3, 50.8]cm)

1" [2.5cm]

9½ (10, 10½, 11)" [24 (25.5, 26.7, 28cm)]

Learning to Hand Dye Multicolored Yarn

Learning to hand dye your own yarn can be a very liberating and creative experience, not to mention lots of fun! This tutorial will cover the basics of hand painting yarn using sock yarn and commercial yarn dyes. The process is very simple, and the results are as limitless as your imagination!

By Adam Church

Skill Level

Intermediate

Materials

- 3½ oz. (100g) of any undyed wool yarn

Samples used for dyeing are:

- Knit Picks *Bare Superwash Merino DK Weight* (100 percent merino wool; 246 yd. [225m] per 3½ oz. [100g] skein): undyed, 1 skein
- Knit Picks *Bare Merino Fingering Weight* (100 percent merino wool; 440 yd. [402.m] per 3½ oz. [100g] skein): undyed, 1 skein

Note The Knit Picks Bare line of undyed yarns was used for this tutorial, as they are ideal yarns for the beginning dyer. Both the Superwash Merino DK Weight and Merino Fingering Weight yarns were used for the sample skeins, but any yarn from the Bare line is suitable.

- Jacquard acid dyes: These dyes are commercial acid dyes, and are used with household vinegar to dye yarn. All of the colors used in the tutorial are available from Knit Picks.
- Measurement utensils
- Latex or rubber gloves
- Dust mask
- Sealable plastic containers
- Household white vinegar
- Disposable cups or bowls
- Foam paint brushes
- Plastic wrap
- Vinyl tablecloth

- Microwave or stock pot with a steaming rack: To set the dyes, the yarn needs to be heated after painting. The yarn can either be heated in a microwave or steamed on the stovetop in a stock pot with a steaming rack.

Safety Considerations

Yarn dyeing is a very safe process provided that a few simple rules are followed.

1. When working with the dye powders wear a dust mask, as the powders are very fine and can be a lung irritant. Once the dye is mixed with water, it is safe to remove the mask. If any dye powder spills on your work surface, use a wet paper towel to wipe up the mess to prevent the dye powder from becoming airborne.

2. Once mixed into liquid form the dyes will stain, so wear latex or rubber gloves to prevent colored fingers. Also, cover your countertop or table with a vinyl tablecloth to prevent staining.

3. All utensils that come into contact with the dyes should be set aside for dyeing only. If an item is only used to measure out water or vinegar, it is safe to use for food preparation. It is also very important to have a heating source (microwave or stock pot) that is only used for yarn dyeing.

4. After your yarn is wrapped and heated, it can be very hot, so be sure to allow ample cool-down time before handling the dyed yarn.

Caution Handling hot yarn without proper precautions can cause moderate to severe burns. Always wear protective gloves and allow the yarn to cool before handling.

Top row: two skeins of Colorway #2, bottom row: two skeins of Colorway #3, far left, one skein of Colorway #1, before reskeining.

Instructions

Project Colorways

The three sample color combinations, as well as the Jacquard acid dye numbers used, are provided to help you get started with the project. However, these colors are only a guideline, so feel free to choose any combination of dyes that you wish.

While the dyeing is done in stripes, you can simply reskein your yarn into a different length or size skein to break up the solid stripes so that the skein looks variegated. Note the contrast above in Colorway #1 on left (before reskeining) and Colorways #2 and #3, after being reskeined.

Mixing the Dyes

The best way to mix up the yarn dyes is to make a 1 percent stock solution. This simply means that there is 1g of dye powder for every 100ml of stock solution. If you have a digital scale that can measure small metric amounts, use that for measuring the powders. Otherwise, the following approximation works well.

1. To make a 1 percent stock solution, mix 1 level teaspoon (3g) of dye powder with approx 1¼ cups (300ml) of hot water.

2. Stir the solution well, making sure that all clumps of dye powder are dissolved. Repeat for each color of dye powder.

Note Be sure to use a sealable container, so that left-over dye solutions can be stored for future dyeing. This solution can be stored up to six months in a dark place. If the dye solution becomes cloudy, simply reheat it in a dye-safe microwave or pot to dissolve the powder.

Dyeing Preparation

1. Soak all the yarn you intend to dye in a sink full of warm (not hot) water for at least 30 minutes.

2. While the yarn is soaking, mix up the dyeing cups and prepare the workspace for dyeing.

To calculate how much dye solution is required, use this simple rule:

Use 1ml of yarn dye solution for each gram of yarn that you are dyeing.

The Knit Picks Bare yarns used in this tutorial are sold as 100g skeins, so 100ml (approx 20 tsp) of stock solution is required to dye each skein. Divide that number (in this case, 100ml) by the number of colors per skein to determine how much dye should be used for each individual color.

Then the dye required per skein is multiplied by the color's "Depth of Shade," a number indicating how dark you want the color to be. The most used depth of shade values are:

¼–½: Pastel Shades

1–1½: Medium Shades

2–3: Dark Shades

For example, all colors in the sample colorways are dyed at a medium shade, except for black, which is dyed at a shade of 2 to give a darker, richer hue. Also, white is considered a color with a shade value of 0.

To illustrate, let's examine Colorway #1. This colorway is composed of 4 colors, so we know that 25ml of dye is required for each color. Then we multiply that amount by the shade value desired for each color, giving 0ml for white, 25ml for chestnut and gold ochre, and 50 ml for black.

Colorway #1			
Color Name	Jacquard Color	Depth of Shade	Dye / Color
White	(No Dye)	0 (No Color)	0ml
Chestnut	80335	1 (Medium)	25ml (5 tsp)
Gold Ochre	80322	1 (Medium)	25ml (5 tsp)
Black	80337	2 (Dark)	50ml (10 tsp)

Colorway #2			
Color Name	Jacquard Color	Depth of Shade	Dye / Color
Emerald	80325	1 (Medium)	35ml (7 tsp)
Chestnut	80335	1 (Medium)	35ml (7 tsp)
Teal	80326	1 (Medium)	35ml (7 tsp)

Colorway #3			
Color Name	Jacquard Color	Depth of Shade	Dye / Color
Purple	80330	1 (Medium)	35ml (7 tsp)
Sapphire Blue	80332	1 (Medium)	35ml (7 tsp)
Gold Ochre	80322	1 (Medium)	35ml (7 tsp)

3. Once you've figured out how much stock solution is needed, measure the required amount for each color into a paper bowl or cup. Then add 1 tablespoon of vinegar, and 250ml (1 cup) of water.

4. Repeat this process to prepare the dyes for each skein of yarn.

Dyeing the Yarn

1. Working with one skein at a time, remove the yarn from the sink and gently squeeze out as much water as possible. Tear off a piece of plastic wrap long enough for the skein to lay on with 6–8" (15–20cm) of space on either end. Lay the plastic wrap on your work surface.

2. Now all you have to do is paint away. Just take a foam brush, dip it in each color, and paint it onto the yarn using an up and down blotting motion.

3. Apply the colors onto the entire skein of yarn, then gently flip the yarn over and repeat on the other side. Using your fingers, inspect the skein for even color coverage, and apply dye to any remaining white spots as necessary. If you run out of dye, just mix up extra cups as necessary, using the original measurements.

4. Once the skein is saturated, soak up any excess water with a paper towel, as this will help the plastic wrap stick to itself better. Fold the bottom half over the yarn, and then the top half over the bottom half. Twist the ends closed and roll the whole package into a coil.

Processing the Yarn

Once the yarn is wrapped up, it is ready to be heated by microwaving or steaming.

Microwaving: Place the yarn in a microwave safe bowl and heat on 50 percent power for 5 minutes. Let it rest for 5 minutes, then heat it again for 5 minutes on 50 percent power.

Steaming: Place the yarn on a steamer rack in a stock pot with 1–2" (2.5–5cm) of water at the bottom. Bring to a boil and steam for around 30 minutes.

Rinsing:

1. After the yarn is heated, wearing latex or rubber gloves, remove it from the heat source and place in a drained sink to cool. *Take care as the yarn will be very hot.* Let the yarn cool to room temperature (this may take a few hours), then rinse in tepid water. It is very important to let the yarn cool to prevent felting and to allow the dye to finish setting.

2. After rinsing, gently squeeze out as much water as possible and hang the yarn to dry.

Finishing: Reskein yarn into a differently sized skein in order to break up stripes and show skein variegation.

Enjoy your beautiful hand-dyed yarn!

Designer Bio

Adam Church is an electrical engineer by day and a fiber enthusiast by night. He runs Yarn Nerd, a company with a scientific twist on hand-dyed yarn, creating unique colors to excite the nerd in everyone. When he's not creating fun colorways such as *Printed Circuit Board*, Adam likes to knit, knit, and knit. His yarns can be found at www.yarnnerd.com.

chapter 2

New York State
Sheep and Wool
Festival

Just after paying my admission to enter the fairgrounds, I see that Rhinebeck—the universally understood code name for the New York State Sheep and Wool Festival, held at the Dutchess County Fairgrounds each October in Rhinebeck, New York—has a lot going on. Nestled between the Catskills and the Berkshires in the Hudson River Valley, Rhinebeck is ablaze with color in the fall, with echoes of mountains in the distance. Even without all the amazing colors on offer at the vendors' stalls, I'm flooded with scenes of the rich hues of autumn.

I don't know if anyone is counting the attendance, but from my point of view, Rhinebeck is probably the second largest festival on the East Coast, or perhaps even in the United States. It's an easy day trip for people from the New York City metropolitan area, and bus loads of eager shoppers come from places like Boston and Cleveland to experience it. What's on offer at Rhinebeck?

This event has all the standard markers of a good festival: lots of amazing shopping opportunities, contests, displays, demonstrations, and even good food and bathrooms. (More on this later. . . .) In particular, there are vendors who attend all the major festivals, as well as vendors like Fiber Kingdom who come only to a few shows, bringing exotic fiber samplers, or The Wool Room, which might host authors doing book signings. These specific details might draw comparisons with other festivals, so here's some of what makes Rhinebeck different.

Rhinebeck is the only festival I attended on the East Coast with a Cashmere goat show, and they're proud of it. Rhinebeck not only has sheep and Angora show competitions, but also a fleece show which has had over 500 fleeces a year. Overwhelmed by the entries, the organizers had to bring in more display tables the year I visited, and the judge worked overtime to finish his work. Meanwhile, participants lined up outside, eager to snatch up high quality fleeces on sale from all over the Northeast.

Across the fairgrounds, there's a different part of the sheep judging world . . . the livestock auction. Just beside the sheep stands and shearing facilities, I entered a building where everything for sale was live. Here, standing behind a teenager wearing a T-shirt that said, "Just Farm It!", I watched prize-winning Tunis ewes and rams auctioned off to the highest bidder. Starting off with the traditional auctioneers' banter, the bidding was quick and efficient. A fellow auctioneer interrupted his colleague in the midst of each sale. "Folks, this is a prize-winning ewe, here, pay attention! Bid her up! This is a good sheep." Almost uniformly, the prices per animal were higher than I'd seen elsewhere. These *were* lovely sheep.

Each year, Rhinebeck has a featured sheep breed, which allows them to have a special sheep show for the breed, and vendors who make sure to carry this particular fiber and yarn in stock. This time, Bluefaced Leicester ruled the show, with everything from hand- and machine-spun yarns to raw fleeces and nearly continuous demonstrations and talks to educate shepherds and the public about this special breed. Vendors created one of a kind hand-dyed yarn spun of Bluefaced Leicester, and Little Barn, a vendor from Alabama, imported British Bluefaced Leicester roving for sale in multiple colors. This wool was everywhere, and it was highly popular.

Eager spinners line up to purchase award-winning fleeces.

Crowds come to Rhinebeck to be well-entertained, and magicians, jugglers, pumpkin carving, straw maze children's attractions, and other delights were the norm. Steam engine and farm equipment displays attracted family members who weren't interested in the many attractive fiber arts wares to be purchased. Also, a Gem and Mineral show shared the grounds, drawing in many shoppers who just happened to have another hobby—beading. The facilities also had a flare that I hadn't seen elsewhere. In an area of the Hudson Valley right near the Culinary Institute of America (the C.I.A., locally), expect food to be top notch. Want kabobs, raviolis, gyros, or tacos made out of lamb? No problem, it's here. Chocolate truffles, cappuccino, fried garlicky artichokes, fresh local cider, apples, and home-made breads were all available. This was also a festival where vegetarians could easily find fair food that was healthy and satisfying, and that's not all.

Festivals often suffer from poor facilities, especially when thousands of women arrive to spend the day, and everyone eventually needs to use the restroom. The Dutchess County Fairgrounds solves this problem in a way that no other festival approaches. There are no porta-potties here. Instead, there are plenty of bathrooms, complete with a full-time attendant who keeps them spotless, plays the radio, greets visitors personally . . . and expects a tip!

Wander over to see the "Make It with Wool" competition and one is bombarded with an astonishing array of fabulously spun, dyed, knitted or woven entries. A fashion show takes place, and I walk by as young teenage girls in braces proudly show off their hip designs, made of wool, of course. Nearby, I meet Miani Carnevale, an artist, and learn about her partner, Judy Malstrom, and their new effort toward building increased community in the area. Miani proudly sits near a sign and growing membership list that says, "Fibre Connection." In her words, "this membership and directory serves to unite fiber farmers and artisans of the Hudson Valley by building community through connection, collaboration, and creativity." I'm struck by how important this effort is, in every fiber arts community, for spinners, knitters, weavers, and shepherds alike.

Informal connections happen everywhere at the fairgrounds with the popular Rhinebeck Blogger Bingo

The featured sheep breed: Bluefaced Leicester.

game. Grab a bingo "card" and keep your eyes peeled for the many bloggers wearing buttons, T-shirts, and other signs. This game's a great chance to greet some of your favorite cyberspace friends in person. On Sunday afternoon, a local bookstore hosts a huge book signing event and one could see famous knitwear designers or even hear the Yarn Harlot, Stephanie Pearl-McPhee, give a special Rhinebeck festival talk.

If the fairground crowds become too much, it's easy enough to make a side trip to see the rural countryside, pick your own apples, or eat at one of the very good restaurants in nearby towns. One can make a trip to Rhinebeck into a mini-vacation!

With perfect fall weather, this weekend brings both profit and joy to an entire community. I was thrilled to visit, and see what all the New Yorkers rave about. Rhinebeck is an experience, and definitely one I'd be sorry to miss.

New York Wine and Cheese

New York State is well known for its Long Island reds and Finger Lake white wines. It's a growing region for wine production. The culture of the state is one that invites people to sit right down and have a locally produced glass of wine (or beer) with their lunch. In fact, the festival announcer invited us all to do so! Throughout the festival, one could visit a winery's stall for a quick wine tasting, or grab a glass of wine with lunch from a festival vendor. Despite the incredibly good libations, I didn't see one person who had managed the situation poorly . . . knitters seem to know that one doesn't drink too much and buy great yarns!

A lesser known fact about New York is its cheese production. Whether it's a local producer such as Sprout Creek Farm in Poughkeepsie, with its goats' and cow's milk cheeses, or the American Cheese Society's booth with its impressive selection, there's a large amount of cheese on hand for tasting. Many festivalgoers grab a chunk of this homemade cheese, a handmade baguette, and some other treats and settle in for lunch with friends. Others purchase lamb (often available from those who sell the sheep's milk cheese) and other farm products, such as maple syrup or honey, to take home as edible souvenirs. New York state is proud of its locally grown, sustainable agriculture, and in this way, the New York State Sheep and Wool Festival becomes something more—a traditional harvest celebration, for city and country dwellers alike.

Festive Fingerless Mitts

These fingerless mitts are the perfect hand-knit accessory to wear to cool autumn sheep and wool festivals. They are quick and easy to knit, and very soft. They feature a Broken Rib pattern with a lacy cuff, crocheted thumb, and picot edging with bead accents. A three-needle bind-off between the mitt and the cuff keeps the cuff lying flat where it belongs. Best of all, they'll keep your hands warm while your fingers remain free to touch and feel yarns and fibers, and make those stash-expanding purchases that always seem to happen at festivals, no matter what the plan might have been!

Designed by Jennifer Tepper Heverly

Skill level

Intermediate

Size

S (M, L, XL)

Finished Circumference

3½ (5, 6½, 8)" (8.9 [12.7, 16.5, 20.3]cm)

Note *The above measurements have quite a bit of negative ease in them due to the rib pattern. The 5" (12.7cm) medium size, for example, will fit a hand approximately 7½" (19cm) around.*

Materials

- 175 yd. (160m) of any fine weight or sport weight yarn that knits up at the appropriate gauge

Sample knit with: Spirit Trail Fiberworks *Uttu* (100 percent Bluefaced Leicester wool; 400 yd. [366m] per 4.85 oz [137.5g] skein): color Soft Teals, 1 skein

- 2 US size 3 (3.25mm) circular needles, 16" (41cm) long, *or size needed to obtain gauge*

  Note *These mitts can be knit on US size 3 (3.25mm) dpns if you prefer.*

- US size D/3 (3.25mm) crochet hook
- Clip stitch marker
- 3 stitch holders
- Tapestry needle

- Beading needle or wire for threading beads onto yarn
- 60 (68, 76, 84) size 6 round or size 5 triangular seed beads to complement yarn color

  Note *There may be beads left over when you are finished. These are maximum amounts to guarantee that you don't run short.*

Gauge

26 sts and 38 rows = 4" (10cm) in St st

Pattern Stitches

Body Pattern

Rnds 1–3: *K2, p1; rep from * to end of rnd.

Rnd 4: Purl.

Rep rnds 1–4 for patt.

Lacy Cuff Pattern

Rnd 1: *P1, k2tog, YO, k1, YO, k2tog; rep from * to end of rnd.

Rnd 2: *P1, k5; rep from * to end of rnd.

Rep rnds 1 and 2 for patt.

Note *These mitts are knit from the palm up towards the wrist. Make both mitts alike. See page 154 for tips on knitting on 2 circular needles.*

Hand

Cast on 39 (45, 51, 57) sts and divide evenly between 2 circular needles. Join, being careful not to twist the sts.

Continue working in Body pattern as est for another 5" (12.7cm)—approx 13 patt repeats—or until mitt reaches desired length, ending after working rnd 4 of patt.

Place sts on 2 stitch holders.

Lacy Cuff

Cast on 42 (48, 54, 60) sts and divide between 2 circular needles, being careful not to twist the sts.

Work 12 rnds of Lacy Cuff pattern.

Work 8 rnds of Body pattern, beg with rnd 4.

Next rnd: *P12 (14, 16, 18) sts, p2tog; rep from * to end of rnd—39 (45, 51, 57) sts rem.

Finishing

Put half of Lacy Cuff sts on a stitch holder, and move half of mitt sts onto a cable needle as follows:

Place mitt sts on the needle so that the center of the thumb hole lines up with the edge of the lace cuff and the lace patt is centered across the palm and the back of the hand.

Make sure that the same number of sts from the mitt and cuff are on the circular needles and stitch holders.

Put cuff over mitt so that the WS of the cuff faces the right side of the mitt, with both circular needles together on one side and both stitch holders together on the other side.

Beg with the circular needle side, work three-needle bind-off (see page 155) across the needles and then across the stitch holders. Loop the end of the yarn through the last st and pull tight.

Clip on a stitch marker to mark the end of the rnd, if desired.

Work in Body pattern until the mitt measures 2" (5cm)—approx 5 patt repeats. End after working rnd 3 of patt.

Thumb Hole

Next rnd: P8, bind off 5 (6, 7, 8) sts, purl to the end of the rnd.

Next rnd: Work 8 sts in patt, cast on 5 (6, 7, 8) sts, work in patt to the end of the rnd.

Crocheted Edging Instructions

Thread 30 (34, 38, 42) beads onto the yarn using a beading needle or a piece of wire wrapped around the yarn.

Note *These instructions may be revised as you crochet based upon your own individual tensioning. The thumb and palm edges should not be too tight, but should be tight enough to keep the mitts snug on the hand. The crocheted edging should not flair out or pucker in from any of the knitted fabric edges. Work the crochet stitches accordingly.*

Note *Crochet with the WS of mitt facing you so the beads align properly to the outside of the mitt.*

Crocheted Picot Edge at Mitt Palm

Beginning on the palm edge, *sc in each of the next 2 cast-on sts, ch1, slip bead, ch1, sl st into last sc, work 1 sc, skip the next cast-on stitch on the mitt; rep from * to the first sc made on palm edge. Slip the yarn end through the last stitch on the crochet hook and pull tight.

Crocheted Picot Edge at Thumb Opening

Rnd 1: Sc around the thumb opening, being careful of spacing so that it is neither too tight, nor too loose.

Rnd 2: *Sc in next 2 sc, ch1, slip bead, ch1, sl st back into the edge where the second sc was just made, sc in next sc, skip the next sc; rep from * to the first sc made on thumb edge. Slip the yarn end through the last stitch on the crochet hook and pull tight.

Crocheted Edge at Lacy Cuff

Beginning at one end of the lace cuff, sc to the center of the first lace scallop, then *sc in each of the next 2 sts, ch1, slip bead, ch1, sl st back into the edge where the second sc was just stitched, sc to the center of the next lace scallop; rep from * until edge has been worked all the way around lace cuff. Slip the yarn end through the last crochet st on the hook and pull tight.

Weave in all ends and block if desired.

Designer Bio

Jennifer Heverly owns Spirit Trail Fiberworks, a company specializing in one-of-a-kind hand-painted yarns, and luxury and rare breed spinning fibers. Her company allows her to join her love of color, fiber, and artistic expression into a vocation that is also an avocation. She knits and spins in Rappahannock County, Virginia, in a handmade house in the woods with her husband, children, and numerous pets. You can visit her online at www.spirit-trail.net and www. thespirittrail.blogspot.com.

Deep V

This deep V-neck sweater is perfect to ward off chills at spring and fall festivals. A quick knit, with slip stitch vertical lines and a double seed stitch edging, you'll find it creates slimming lines. Designed with a double strand of organic cotton in mind, this can also be transformed into winter wear in wool. Set-in sleeves cut down on unnecessary bulk around the shoulders. With a three-quarter length that allows you easy access to festival finds, there'll be no need to push up your sleeves for serious shopping!

Skill level

Easy

Size

XS (S, M, L)

Finished Bust: 36 (40, 44, 48)" (91.5 [102, 112, 122]cm)

Materials

Note This sweater can be made with a double strand of worsted weight yarn or a single strand of bulky weight yarn.

- 1,625 (1,625; 1,950; 1,950) yd. (1,486 [1,486; 1,783; 1,783]m) of any worsted weight yarn that knits up with the appropriate gauge when knitting with 2 strands held together

or

- 813 (813, 975, 975) yd. (744 [744, 892, 892]m) of any bulky weight yarn that knits up with the appropriate gauge when knitting with 1 strand

Sample knit with: Decadent Fibers *Spumoni* (100 percent organic cotton; 325 yd. [297m] per 8 oz. [227g] skein): color Vanilla, 5 (5, 6, 6) skeins (used double stranded)

- US size 10 (6mm) circular needle, 29" (74cm) long, *or size to obtain gauge*
- US size 10 (6mm) straight needles (optional)
- Stitch holders
- Row marker
- Tapestry needle

Gauge

Using a double strand of worsted weight yarn or a single strand of bulky weight yarn:

12 sts and 20 rows = 4" (10cm) in St st

14½ sts and 22 rows = 4" (10cm) in Vertical Slip Stitch

13 sts and 20 rows = 4" (10cm) in Double Seed Stitch

Pattern Stitches

Double Seed Stitch

May be worked over a multiple of 4 + 2 or an even multiple of 4 sts.

Row 1 (RS): *K2, p2; rep from * to last 2 sts, k2.

Row 2: Knit the purl sts and purl the knit sts.

Rep rows 1 and 2 for patt.

Note When working over an even multiple of 4, omit the last 2 sts at the end of row 1.

Vertical Slip Stitch

Worked over an even number of sts.

Row 1 (RS): *K1, sl1 knitwise; rep from * across.

Row 2: Purl.

Repeat Rows 1 and 2 for patt.

Instructions

Note Slip the last st of each row purlwise wyif for a neat edge.

When only 1 number is listed, it is applicable for all sizes.

Back

With 2 strands of worsted weight yarn or 1 strand of bulky yarn and circular or straight needles, cast on 66 (74, 82, 90) sts.

Work in Double Seed Stitch for 6 (6, 8, 8) rows.

Work in Vertical Slip Stitch until Back measures 15 (15½, 17, 17)" (38 [39.5, 43, 43]cm).

Shape armhole

BO 6 (6, 8, 8) sts at the beg of the next 2 rows.

Work in Vertical Slip Stitch as est until the armhole measures 7 (8, 8½, 9)" (17.8 [20.3, 21.6, 22.9]cm), ending after a WS row.

Shape neck

Next row (RS): Work 14 (16, 18, 20) sts in patt, bind off 26 (30, 30, 34) sts, work rem 14 (16, 18, 20) sts in patt.

Shoulders

Next row (WS): Turn and work across first 14 (16, 18, 20) sts on the needle, leaving rem sts for second shoulder to be worked later.

Work even in pattern as est on 14 (16, 18, 20) sts for 2 (2, 2½, 2½)" (5 [5, 6.4, 6.4]cm) or until total armhole depth is 9 (10, 11, 11½)" (22.9 [25.4, 27.9, 29.2]cm).

Bind off.

With WS facing, attach 2 strands of worsted weight yarn or 1 strand of bulky weight yarn to other shoulder at neck edge. Beg on a WS row, work as first shoulder.

Front

Work the same as Back until Front measures 12 (12½, 14, 14)" (30.5 [31.8, 35.5, 35.5]cm), ending after a WS row.

Shape V neck

Next row (RS): Work 26 (30, 33, 37) sts in Vertical Slip Stitch as est, bind off 14 (14, 16, 16) sts, work remaining 26 (30, 33, 37) sts in patt.

Next row (WS): Turn and work across first 26 (30, 33, 37) sts. Put remaining 26 (30, 33, 37) sts on holder for second shoulder to be worked later.

*Work 3 rows even.

Next row (WS): Dec 1 st at neck edge.

Dec 1 at neck edge every 6 rows 2 times—23 (27, 30, 34) sts rem.

At the same time, when Front measures 15 (15½, 17, 17)" (38 [39.5, 43]cm), bind off 6 (6, 8, 8) sts at armhole edge.

Dec 1 st at neck edge every 6 (4, 6, 4) rows 3 (5, 4, 6) times.

Work rem 14 (16,18,20) sts until total armhole depth measures 9 (10, 11, 11½)" (22.9 [25.4, 27.9, 29.2]cm).

Bind off.

With WS facing, attach 2 strands of worsted weight yarn or 1 strand of bulky weight yarn to other shoulder at neck edge. Purl 1 row, then work as first shoulder from *.

Back

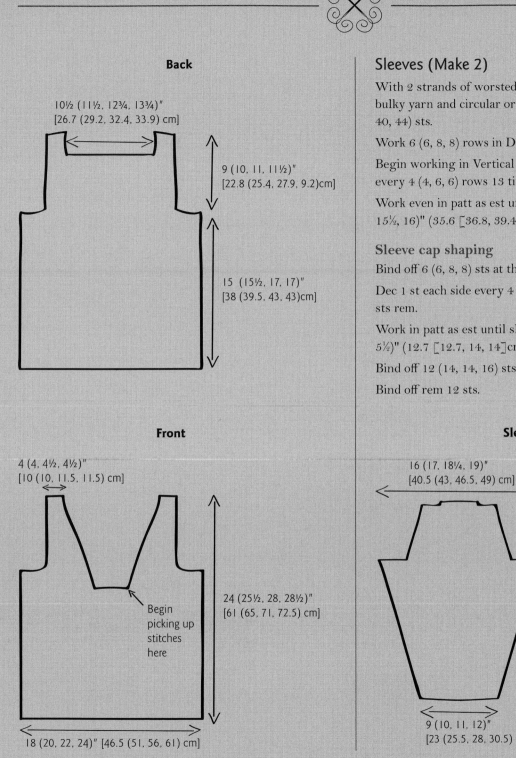

10½ (11½, 12¾, 13¾)"
[26.7 (29.2, 32.4, 33.9) cm]

9 (10, 11, 11½)"
[22.8 (25.4, 27.9, 9.2)cm]

15 (15½, 17, 17)"
[38 (39.5, 43, 43)cm]

Front

4 (4, 4½, 4½)"
[10 (10, 11.5, 11.5) cm]

Begin picking up stitches here

24 (25½, 28, 28½)"
[61 (65, 71, 72.5) cm]

18 (20, 22, 24)" [46.5 (51, 56, 61) cm]

Sleeves (Make 2)

With 2 strands of worsted weight yarn or 1 strand of bulky yarn and circular or straight needles, cast on 32 (36, 40, 44) sts.

Work 6 (6, 8, 8) rows in Double Seed Stitch.

Begin working in Vertical Slip Stitch, inc 1 st each side every 4 (4, 6, 6) rows 13 times—58 (62, 66, 70) sts.

Work even in patt as est until sleeve measures 14 (14½, 15½, 16)" (35.6 [36.8, 39.4, 40.6]cm).

Sleeve cap shaping

Bind off 6 (6, 8, 8) sts at the beg of the next 2 rows.

Dec 1 st each side every 4 rows 5 times—36 (40, 40, 44) sts rem.

Work in patt as est until sleeve cap measures 5 (5, 5½, 5½)" (12.7 [12.7, 14, 14]cm).

Bind off 12 (14, 14, 16) sts at the beg of the next 2 rows.

Bind off rem 12 sts.

Sleeve

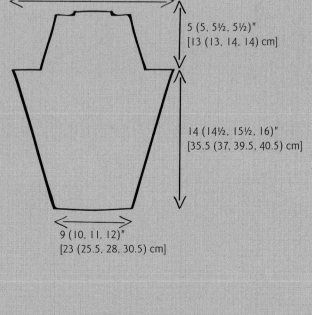

16 (17, 18¼, 19)"
[40.5 (43, 46.5, 49) cm]

5 (5, 5½, 5½)"
[13 (13, 14, 14) cm]

14 (14½, 15½, 16)"
[35.5 (37, 39.5, 40.5) cm]

9 (10, 11, 12)"
[23 (25.5, 28, 30.5) cm]

Finishing

Using only 1 strand of yarn and a tapestry needle, sew shoulder seams. Folding sleeve in half, align the tip of the sleeve cap with shoulder seam. Sew the set-in sleeve seams and side seams.

V-neck Collar

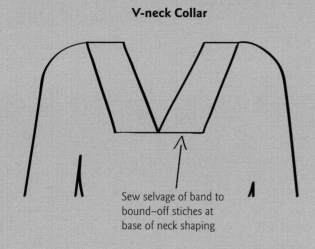

Sew selvage of band to bound–off stiches at base of neck shaping

V-neck Collar

Using circular needle and starting at the right edge of the V neck, (see arrow in schematic at left) pick up and knit 30 (34, 36, 37) sts on first side of v neck, 34 (38, 40, 44) sts across back neck, and 30 (34, 36, 37) sts on second side of V-neck—94 (106, 112, 118) sts total.

Note *The exact number of sts is not crucial but you need an even number of sts for the patt. Here's a guideline to follow: You should have approximately 3 sts for every 4 rows.*

Work 8 (8, 10, 10) rows of Double Seed Stitch patt.

Bind off in patt.

When flat, the collar selvage edges should meet at the center of the V neck as shown. Sew collar selvage edges securely to the flat V-neck bind-off.

Wash and dry flat to block.

The Curious Ewe

This rug hooking project is small so as to encourage a beginner to take on something new. The wool samples are all from recycled clothing which can be found at secondhand or thrift stores or even in one's own closet. Rug hooking is a traditional American craft which started in the early 1800s and allowed folk artists to make rugs and art hangings that offer warmth and decoration. Although new wool fabric can be used, making art out of scraps and shreds of old textiles has always been economical and a great way to recycle and protect the environment. Primitive rug hooking is often on display at fiber festivals, and Rug Hooking Magazine recognizes New York State Sheep and Wool Festival as a particular favorite.

Hooked on Ewe's Linda Harwood often focuses on sheep in her rugs. She says her inspiration for this piece, with its ewe and butterfly, came from her farm upbringing: "Having lived on a farm my entire life, I can appreciate how curious sheep can be. I have often seen them nose to nose trying to figure something out."

Designed by Linda Harwood

Skill level

Easy

Finished Measurements

17½ × 13½" (44.5 × 34.3cm)

Materials

- Coarse rug hook (for wide strips)
- 14" (35.5cm) heavy wooden hoop or embroidery frame to keep pattern tight
- Burlap or linen backing made especially for rug hooking
- Washed wool fabric in the following amounts and colors:

  Sheep body 27 × 9" (68.6 × 22.9cm), off white

  Head and legs 15 × 3" (38 × 7.6cm), brown

  Butterfly light 5 × 8" (12.7 × 20.3cm), yellow

  Butterfly dark 10 × 7" (25.4 × 17.8cm), gold

  Butterfly body 3 × ¼" (7.6 × .6cm), black

  Stem and leaves 41 × 1½" (104.1 × 3.8cm), green

  Berries 14 × 1½" (35.6 × 3.8cm), red

  Background 45 × 18" (114.3 × 45.7cm), purple

  Border 54 × 18" (137.2 × 45.7cm), burgundy

  Note These amounts provide enough fabric to layer the wool 5 times over the space that is to be hooked.

- Rug hook fabric-strip cutter or sharp fabric scissors

  Note You do not need a cutter; you can cut your strips by hand. Always cut on the straight grain of the material. Cutters are much easier and faster but the first hooked rugs were cut by hand and not all strips were perfectly cut.

- Copy machine or graph paper
- Permanent marker
- Steam iron and white towel
- Sewing machine and sewing thread
- 2 yd. (1.8m) of cotton twill rug tape
- Heavy-duty hand-sewing needle and thread
- Dowel (optional for hanging rug)

Where to Get Wool Fabrics for Hooking

The Curious Ewe is hooked with recycled wool material, wool you would find in secondhand stores or your own closet. I find it fun to look at men's beautiful tweed jackets and visualize them hooked. Using plaids, tweeds, and checks adds rich texture and character to hooked pieces. The ewe itself is hooked with two different tweeds.

Instructions

Preparation

1. Cut the fabric into strips that are #6 cut (³/₁₆" [4.7mm] wide) or #7 cut (⁷/₃₂" [5.5mm] wide).
2. Enlarge the pattern on page 34 to 17½ × 13½" (44.5 × 34.3cm) using a copy machine or graph paper (enlarge by approximately 275%).
3. Using a permanent marker, transfer the design to the burlap or linen backing, allowing yourself a 2–3" (5.1–7.6cm) border around the pattern on the backing. Make sure you have drawn the pattern on straight.

Hooking the Rug

Start at the top of the design so you keep the shape of the design. For example, the butterfly is on the top of the stem so hook the butterfly first. Hook just inside the lines.

Put the part of the pattern that you are planning to start within the hoop.

Begin hooking as follows, using the illustrations as a guide.

1. Tuck the hoop in the crook of your left arm. In your left hand hold the end of the fabric strip between your thumb and forefinger under the pattern. In your right hand, hold the hook on top of the pattern.

2. Go down and bring up the strip of wool being careful not to let strips twist and do not cross over any hooking.

3. Start by bringing the first strip up on top with the end showing (all ends should be on the top and cut off even with the top of the loops later when hooked piece is finished).

4. Do not pack your loops tightly together; they should gently touch each other with no backing showing.

5. Bring up each loop to the height of the strip. (You can check the height by laying a cut strip on its side next to the loops.)

6. Outline what you plan to hook first and then fill it in. Always hook nice straight lines around your outer edge.

7. Hook your background color around designs but before filling in the entire background, jump ahead and hook the border.

8. Continue hooking until finished.

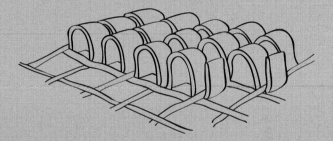

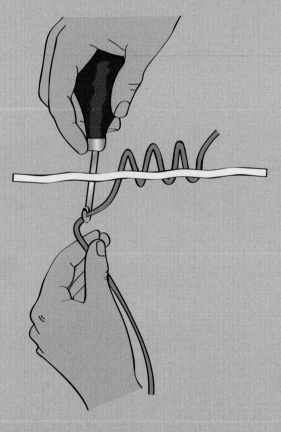

Finishing

When your piece is finished, press the back of your rug with lots of steam and a white towel and let dry. Then press the front in the same way.

You are now ready to bind the edges of your rug.

1. With the sewing machine, zigzag 2 to 3 times around the edges of your hooking.

2. Using cotton twill rug tape and heavy thread, whip stitch close to the last roll of hooking so no backing shows, then trim off extra backing and sew the tape to the back.

3. If you choose to hang your piece, you can put a dowel at the top of rug by inserting the dowel before whip stitching the tape at the top of the rug. Alternately, you can use matching tape to add loops on the WS, at the top of the rug, for inserting the dowel for hanging.

Designer's Bio

Linda Harwood taught herself the art of rug hooking and runs her own business, Hooked on Ewe. Some of her inspiration is drawn from the old world, from animals and her country background. Linda teaches, makes kits, and does commission work. You can view some of her work at www.harwoodhookedonewe.com.

chapter 3

New Hampshire
Sheep and Wool
Festival

It's bright, sunny and cool in New Hampshire the second week of May, although as with any festival, it can run the risk of a spring rainstorm. Even before hitting the festival, I'm serenaded by Chorus frogs and treated to scenic views of historic hydro-powered textile mills which remind me of New Hampshire's rich textile traditions. First thing in the morning, my car enters the festival gates behind a truck with Maine license plates. In the front seat, the border collies beside the driver prance and shimmy, excited to see the sheep that have been brought in for the sheep dog trials that will take place during the festival.

The New Hampshire fair grounds are big, filled with tall pine trees, barns and outbuildings. There's a small museum on the site, and multiple gates to enter on festival days. The atmosphere is relaxed, open and friendly. Unlike the crowds of excited shoppers at Maryland, in New Hampshire, there's room to spread out.

There are large quantities of animals, hidden in barns among the trees. Children are everywhere, working intently, getting their animals ready to be shown and seen. The alpaca and llama areas are particularly full, with the buzz of a New England Alpaca Owners and Breeds Association event happening at the same time. Alpaca owners talk with friends and ask detailed questions of spinners, knitters and other passersby, engaging everyone in fascinating conversation. For the first time, I see Suri alpacas in person and hear alpacas of all colors whistle, squeak and grunt. One big luxuriously rich white colored male even begins to spit as he sees people walk by!

Inside the fairground buildings, I'm invited in to see the Grafton Fibers intricate dyed batts and needle felted dragons, the woodwork of the Merlin Tree's HitchHiker wheels, the Vermont Wheel, and the Bosworth's Journey Wheels and spindles—all New England-made. The richness of the fibers is unparalleled; the view up close is uncrowded and calm. A batt of royal blue, kelly green, and ebony hops off Graton Fibers' shelves and into my hands. It's coming home with me.

For lunch, there are more firsts to sample. Lobster rolls from one vendor, and New England style Indian pudding and apple crisp with ice cream from another vendor, Belgian Acres Farm, are all on the menu. Indian pudding, a mixture of corn meal, molasses, and spices similar to those used in pumpkin pie, is a filling new treat. The warm pudding and apple crisp are accented by the cold vanilla ice cream, and all slide down smoothly as fairgoers share picnic tables, conversation and tips. Strangers strike up conversations in moments of mutual admiration for an animal, technique, or experience.

Kisakanari Farms boasts Jacob sheep fleeces, and the owner takes time to show me her technique for spinning raw fleeces, and how she made an enormous multi-colored Elizabeth Zimmerman Pi Shawl that is on display. She insists that she's taught her dogs to stay away from the tantalizing odors of freshly shorn fleece, but I doubt mine will learn this skill! There's time and space at this event to have a chat and to do one-on-one demonstrations. I'm drawn away to see buttons made out of deer antlers and Jacobs' sheep horn.

Alive with color: Grafton Fibers' Corriedale batts for felters and spinners.

Meanwhile, teenagers lead their llamas and alpacas through complicated obstacle courses, complete with steps, a balance beam, and other challenges. When the alpacas shy away from the balance beam, I see young girls leave the ring looking frustrated and unhappy. It takes patience and skill to guide an animal through this maneuver, but in all cases, these young people, enthusiastic about fiber arts and animals, are treated with respect and enthusiasm by the adults in the crowd.

Nearby, there are informal tutorials on how to wash a fleece, how to judge good and bad fleece, and how to produce delicious meat for your freezer from your meat sheep. A young man plays banjo for tips, and the international sheep dog trials continue in earnest all day long.

What's NEAOBA?

The New England Alpaca Owners and Breeders Association (NEAOBA) educates and aides many alpaca and llama owners in New England. This is a community that looks forward to the New Hampshire Sheep and Wool Festival each year as a chance to visit, learn, and share ideas, as well as to sell fiber, yarns, products and animals. While many of these small alpaca farm owners will have animals competing against one another throughout the year, at this event, everyone is cooperative and friendly.

Special free seminars educate passersby and farm owners alike on how to market one's farm or how to spin alpaca. Tips about the drapey, silky, inelastic nature of alpaca and its best uses in spinning and knitting abound. Every farmer's stall is filled with special animals and everyone is invited in to meet the animals and their fiber.

Small farm producers find a market at festivals like this. You may find a one-of-a-kind item. Small runs of naturally colored alpaca and llama yarns, identified by the name of the animal and the farm are especially precious and hard to purchase anywhere but at a festival like this one.

Destiny's Farm offers both alpaca fleece and yarns straight from the farm.

West Mountain Farm's llamas pose for the camera.

An antique Shaker great wheel is on display.

Children and adults crowd around to see spinning and weaving demonstrations. The antique Shaker great wheel is a particular hit, and the beautifully spun, woven, knit or crocheted textiles done by local fiber artists decorate the hall for all to see. In another building, the annual sheep to shawl competition begins, with both adult and children's teams competing in costume.

A group of adults dressed as the Mad Hatter's tea party from Alice in Wonderland smile their way through the rushed spinning and weaving event, creating an admirable shawl. Meanwhile the pint-sized sprites and pixies from the Community Shepherd's 4-H club take their task very seriously and produce a skilled finished product. They spin and weave a magical scarf using pastel colored wool and drinking straws as part of their loom warp. Each building is a small oasis of shade, a bit cooler but not quiet. The walls reverberate with laughter, the buzz of conversation, the baaas of local sheep, and the shrieks of children.

The sun begins to warm me up, and I leave the fairgrounds sated and tired. A country store comes into view, and I'm invited in to get small gifts of maple sugar and syrup. I travel on to a small New Hampshire village, and wander the small shops, rewarded with much larger bottles of maple syrup, made locally. Several others stop to tell me this is indeed good syrup. I have no doubt. The Yankee tradition of honestly kind and brisk hospitality has its own warmth and unique charm.

Apple Crisp Recipe

Here's a very flexible recipe so you can simulate your own fiber festival treat at home whenever you need a fix! Serve with vanilla ice cream, whipped cream or fresh cream if you feel it's necessary, or just eat it on its own. It's good enough naked.

The Filling

2 lbs apples (mix a couple of varieties for best flavor) This is roughly 6 apples, but cut up as many as fit in your pan. Core the apples. Peel if desired.* Chop into pieces.

½ cup brown sugar

2 Tablespoons lemon juice (optional)

½ teaspoon lemon peel (optional)

The Crisp/Crumbly Bits

¾ cup white flour

¼ cup corn meal

¼ cup oatmeal (regular or quick)

¼ cup brown sugar

½ stick (¼ cup) butter or margarine

½ cup coarsely chopped nuts such as walnuts, pecans or hazelnuts (optional)

½ teaspoon cinnamon

¼ teaspoon nutmeg (optional)

¼ teaspoon cloves (optional)

¼ teaspoon allspice (optional)

Preheat oven to 375° F. (350 or 400° is ok if you're cooking something else at the same time.) Grease an 8 or 9 inch baking pan with a little of the butter or margarine. Put the chopped up apples into the pan. Sprinkle in the brown sugar, optional lemon juice, and peel and gently toss the apples until coated.

In a separate bowl, combine all the dry crisp ingredients. Melt the butter or margarine and mix it together with the dry ingredients until it looks like coarse meal. Sprinkle topping evenly over the apples. (You can make this ahead to this point, but be sure to use lemon juice to keep the apples from going brown.)

Note (Food Processor version) If you have appliances and are short on time, throw all the dry crisp ingredients except the nuts into your food processor and pulse once or twice. Throw in butter or margarine in 1 Tablespoon chunks. Pulse. Add nuts. Pulse briefly.

Sprinkle the topping evenly over the apples. Bake for 30 to 40 minutes, until apples have softened and topping is brown.

Variations: Don't have enough apples? This crisp works well with fruit combinations. Try apples and raspberries or strawberries. Peaches, Pears, and Apricots are also nice. Be creative.

*For increased fiber and extra vitamins, don't peel. (This *is* a book about fiber, right?)

Unmistakably Warm Cowl

This quick neck gaiter uses just one skein of alpaca yarn and it's very flexible. The Mistake Rib pattern stretches to fit either a man or a woman, and adds textured detail to a cold weather essential. Use wool if you prefer a more elastic neck warmer with less drape, or use a thicker yarn if you live in a particularly cold climate. Tuck this cowl into your pocket just in case and keep it handy to cover your neck, ears, or hair. It's perfect to fight off a chilly day at any sheep and wool festival!

Skill level

Easy

Size

One size fits any adult head

Finished Measurements

Circumference: 20" (51cm), unstretched
Length: 5" (12.5cm)

Materials

- 115 yd. (105m) of any light weight or DK weight yarn with the appropriate gauge for a lacy texture

or

- 115 yd. (105m) of a worsted weight yarn that will knit up at the same gauge for a denser, warmer cowl

Sample is knit with: Honey Lane Farms *DK Weight Heathered Alpaca Yarn* (100% alpaca, 115 yd. [105m] per 1-3/4 oz. [50g] skein: color Forrest Green, 1 skein)

- US size 9 (5.5mm) circular needle, 24" (61cm) long *or size needed to obtain gauge*

- Stitch marker

- Tapestry needle

Gauge

16 sts and 20 rnds = 4" (10cm) in St st

Pattern Stitches

K4, P2 Ribbing

Worked over a multiple of 6.

Every Rnd: *K4, p2; rep from * to end of rnd.

Mistake Stitch Rib

Worked over a multiple of 4 + 3.

Rnd 1: *K2, p2; rep from *, to last 3 sts, k2, p1.

Rnd 2: P1, *k2, p2; rep from * to last 2 sts, k2.

Rep rnds 1 and 2 for patt.

Instructions

Cast on 90 sts. Join, taking care not to twist sts, and place marker.

Work 1" (2.5cm) or 5 rnds in k4, p2 ribbing. In the last round, dec 3 sts evenly around—87 sts rem.

Switch to Mistake Stitch Rib and work even until piece measures 4" (10cm) from beg.

Return to k4, p2 ribbing, inc 3 sts evenly across first round—90 sts.

Work 1" (2.5cm) or 5 rows. Piece should measure approx 5" (12.5cm).

Bind off loosely in patt.

Finishing

Weave in ends.

Block lightly, if desired. In order to maintain the elasticity of the ribbing, do not stretch or pin in shape. Dry flat.

Natural Alpaca Ruana

This ruana is elegant and truly sumptuous to wear. With multiple shades of naturally colored alpaca yarn, this is the ultimate in natural fiber fashion and luxury. Wrap yourself in this and be warm and ready for a night on the town—or a leisurely spring or fall stroll outdoors.

Designed by Annie Modesitt

Skill level

Intermediate

Size

1 Size

Finished Measurements

When Blocked, Ruana Back measures 44" (111.8cm) wide; length from back point to front point measures 60" (152.4cm).

Materials

- Sport weight alpaca yarn that knits up at the appropriate gauge in a variety of colors:

    A: 880 yd. (800m)

    B: 440 yd. (400m)

    C: 440 yd. (400m)

    D: 550 yd. (500m)

    E: 330 yd. (300m)

    F: 330 yd. (300m)

    Sample is knit with: Blue Sky Alpacas, Sport Weight (100 percent baby alpaca; 110 yd. [100m] per 1¾ oz. [50g] skein):

    A: #509 Natural Dk Gray, 8 balls

    B: #508 Natural Med Gray, 4 balls

    C: #507 Natural Lt Gray, 4 balls

    D: #501 Natural Dk Brown, 5 balls

    E: #502 Natural Copper, 3 balls

    F: #503 Natural Med Tan, 3 balls

- US size 9 (5.5mm) straight needles or circular needle
- US size I-9 (5.5mm) crochet hook
- Tapestry needle

Gauge

16 sts and 24 rows = 4" (10cm) in garter stitch

Note *Gauge is not vital for this project.*

Pattern Stitches and Techniques

VDD (vertical double decrease)

Sl2 sts as if to k2tog, k1, pass slipped sts over (2 sts dec).

Twisted Float Trim

Working on WS, but keeping strands to RS of work, with current color [CC] k1, drop strand, (bring strand of new color [NC] over hanging strand of CC, with NC k1, bring strand of CC over strand of NC, with CC k1) rep to last st. Break CC.

Rev sc (crab st)

Working from left to right, insert crochet hook in next st to the right, YO, draw through st, complete as for sc.

Crochet seam

Insert hook in 1 layer of fabric, then push hook through next layer of fabric to be joined to first. YO hook. Pull yarn through both layers of fabric. YO hook. Pull yarn through 2 loops on hook (1 sc made).

Join new ball of yarn

Work next st with new yarn, work following st with tail only of new yarn. Work all subsequent sts with live end of new yarn.

Weave in ends while knitting

Work 1 st (wrap ends to be woven in around live yarn, then work next st with live yarn). Rep 6 times, or until you feel the tails are woven in securely. It may be necessary to slightly stretch the fabric to keep the woven strands from creating a gather.

Instructions

Note *Read all instructions before beginning.*

Back

Initial Layer of Diamonds

Mitered Diamond #1 (make 9)

Following the chart for Mitered Diamond #1, work with colors A, E, D as follows:

With A, cast on 33 sts.

Row 1 (WS): K16, p1, k to end.

Row 2 (RS): K to 1 st before center st, VDD, k to end.

Row 3 (WS): K to center st, p1, k to end.

Repeat last 2 rows until 27 sts rem on needle, change to E.

Cont working as est until 13 sts rem on needle, change to D.

Work until 1 st rem, fasten off.

Nesting Layer of 8 Diamonds

In this layer, and every subsequent even layer of diamonds, you will join the diamonds from the previous layer by creating 1 fewer diamond than in the previous layer.

Following the chart for Mitered Diamond #1, work with colors A, E, D as follows:

With A, pick up and k17 sts along the left edge of 1 diamond. Working on the same needle and cont with A, pick up and k17 sts along the right edge of the next diamond.

Row 1 (WS): K16, p2tog, k to end—33 sts.

Row 2 (RS): K to 1 st before center st, VDD, k to end.

Row 3 (WS): K to center st, p1, k to end.

Repeat last 2 rows until 27 sts rem on needle, change to E.

Cont working as est until 13 sts rem on needle, change to D.

Work until 1 st rem, fasten off.

Nesting Layer of 9 Diamonds

In this layer, and every subsequent odd layer of diamonds, you will join the diamonds from the previous layer by creating 1 more diamond than in previous layer.

Mitered Diamond I

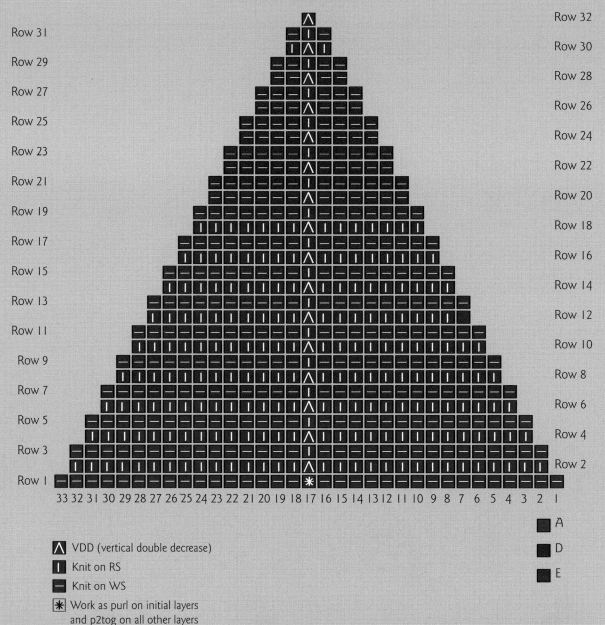

/\	VDD (vertical double decrease)
I	Knit on RS
−	Knit on WS
✳	Work as purl on initial layers and p2tog on all other layers

A

D

E

Right Edge Diamond:

With A, cast on 17 sts. Working on the same needle and cont with A, pick up and k17 sts along the right edge of the next diamond.

Row 1 (WS): K16, p2tog, k to end—33 sts.

Row 2 (RS): K to 1 st before center st, VDD, k to end.

Row 3 (WS): K to center st, p1, k to end.

Repeat last 2 rows until 27 sts rem on needle, change to D.

Cont working as est until 13 sts rem on needle, change to B.

Work until 1 st rem, fasten off.

Center Diamonds:

With A, pick up and k17 sts along the left edge of 1 diamond, working on the same needle and cont with A, pick up and k17 sts along the right edge of the next diamond—34 sts total.

Row 1 (WS): K16, p2tog, k to end—33 sts.

Row 2 (RS): K to 1 st before center st, VDD, k to end.

Row 3 (WS): K to center st, p1, k to end.

Repeat last 2 rows until 27 sts rem on needle, change to D.

Cont working as est until 13 sts rem on needle, change to B.

Work until 1 st rem, fasten off.

Left Edge Diamond:

With A, pick up and k17 sts along the left edge of the last diamond worked, then cast on 17 sts on the same needle using whatever cast on method you prefer.

Row 1 (WS): K16, p2tog, k to end—33 sts.

Row 2 (RS): K to 1 st before center st, VDD, k to end.

Row 3 (WS): K to center st, p1, k to end.

Repeat last 2 rows until 27 sts rem on needle, change to D.

Cont working as est until 13 sts rem on needle, change to B.

Work until 1 st rem, fasten off.

Cont working as est, alternating 9-diamond odd layers and 8-diamond even layers as shown in schematic until a total of 10 layers have been worked, with the specified colors as follows:

Layer 1: Establishing layer of 9 diamonds worked in A, E, D

Layer 2: Layer of 8 diamonds in A, E, D

Layer 3: Layer of 9 diamonds in A, D, B

Layer 4: Layer of 8 diamonds in A, D, B

Layer 5: Layer of 9 diamonds in A, B, C

Layer 6: Layer of 8 diamonds in A, B, C

Layer 7: Layer of 9 diamonds in A, B, D

Layer 8: Layer of 8 diamonds in A, B, D

Layer 9: Layer of 9 diamonds in A, B, C

Layer 10: Layer of 8 diamonds in A, B, C

Final Diamond:

Work 1 diamond between diamonds 4 & 5 of previous layers in A, B, C.

Front (make 2 pieces alike)

Initial Front Diamond

Following the chart for Mitered Diamond #1, work with colors A, F, E as follows:

With A, cast on 33 sts.

Row 1 (WS): K16, p1, k to end.

Row 2 (RS): K to 1 st before center st, VDD, k to end.

Row 3 (WS): K to center st, p1, k to end.

Repeat last 2 rows until 27 sts rem on needle, change to F.

Cont working as est until 13 sts rem on needle, change to E.

Work until 1 st rem, fasten off.

Layer 2 Right Edge Front Diamond

With A, cast on 17 sts. Working on the same needle and cont with A, pick up and k17 sts along the right edge of the initial Front Diamond.

Follow the chart for Mitered Diamond #1, work with colors A, E, D.

Layer 2 Left Edge Diamond

With A, pick up and k17 sts along the left edge of the initial Front Diamond, then cast on 17 sts on the same needle using whatever cast on method you prefer.

Follow the chart for Mitered Diamond #1, work with colors A, E, D.

Layer 3 Right Edge Front Diamond

With A, cast on 17 sts. Working on the same needle and cont with A, pick up and k17 sts along the right edge of the layer 2 Right Edge Diamond.

Follow the chart for Mitered Diamond #1, work with colors A, E, D.

Layer 3 Left Edge Diamond

With A, pick up and k17 sts along the left edge of the layer 2 Left Edge Diamond, then cast on 17 sts on the same needle using whatever cast on method you prefer.

Follow the chart for Mitered Diamond #1, work with colors A, E, D.

Layer 4 Right Edge Front Diamond

With A, cast on 17 sts. Working on the same needle and cont with A, pick up and k17 sts along the right edge of the layer 3 Right Edge Diamond.

Follow the chart for Mitered Diamond #1, work with colors A, B, C.

Mitered Diamond 2
Small Twisted Float

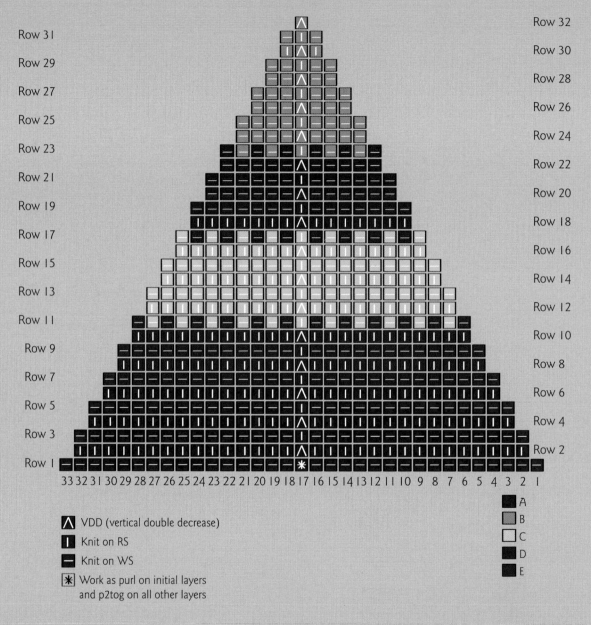

Row 31   Row 32
          Row 30
Row 29   Row 28
Row 27   Row 26
Row 25   Row 24
Row 23   Row 22
Row 21   Row 20
Row 19   Row 18
Row 17   Row 16
Row 15   Row 14
Row 13   Row 12
Row 11   Row 10
Row 9   Row 8
Row 7   Row 6
Row 5   Row 4
Row 3   Row 2
Row 1

33 32 31 30 29 28 27 26 25 24 23 22 21 20 19 18 17 16 15 14 13 12 11 10 9 8 7 6 5 4 3 2 1

∧ VDD (vertical double decrease)

I Knit on RS

— Knit on WS

✳ Work as purl on initial layers
   and p2tog on all other layers

■ A
■ B
□ C
■ D
■ E

Mitered Diamond 3
Double Twisted Float Diamond

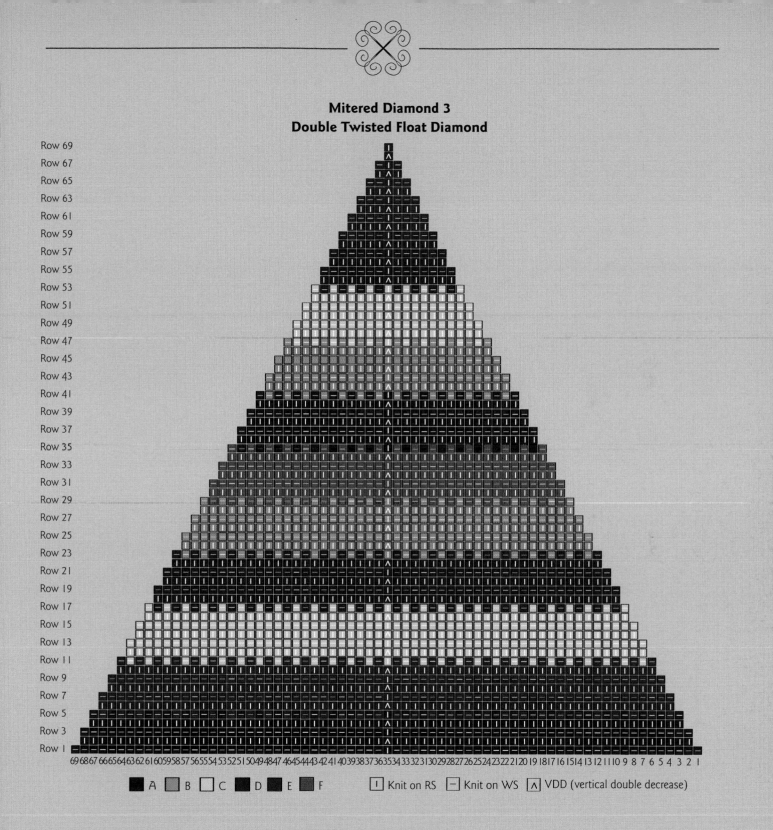

Row 69
Row 67
Row 65
Row 63
Row 61
Row 59
Row 57
Row 55
Row 53
Row 51
Row 49
Row 47
Row 45
Row 43
Row 41
Row 39
Row 37
Row 35
Row 33
Row 31
Row 29
Row 27
Row 25
Row 23
Row 21
Row 19
Row 17
Row 15
Row 13
Row 11
Row 9
Row 7
Row 5
Row 3
Row 1

69 68 67 66 65 64 63 62 61 60 59 58 57 56 55 54 53 52 51 50 49 48 47 46 45 44 43 42 41 40 39 38 37 36 35 34 33 32 31 30 29 28 27 26 25 24 23 22 21 20 19 18 17 16 15 14 13 12 11 10 9 8 7 6 5 4 3 2 1

A ■ B ■ C □ D ■ E ■ F ■   │ Knit on RS   − Knit on WS   ∧ VDD (vertical double decrease)

Mitered Ruana Layout

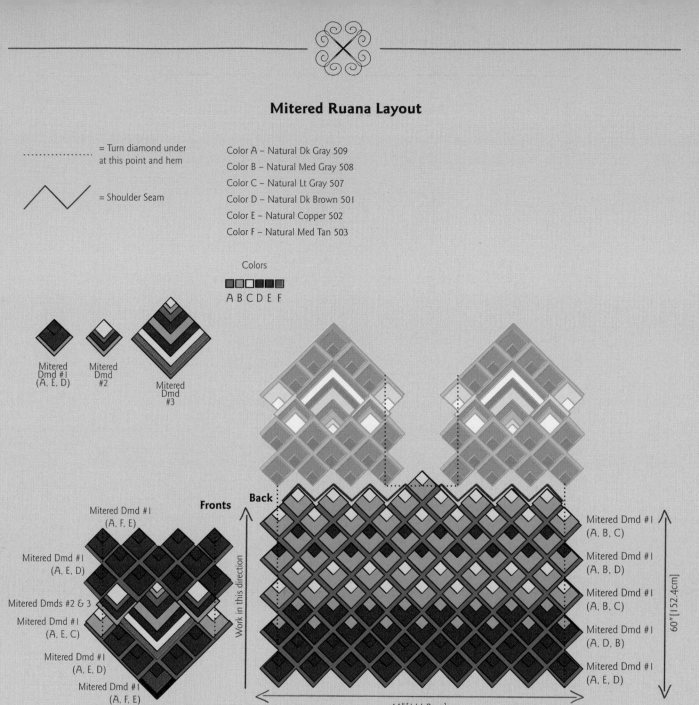

·············· = Turn diamond under at this point and hem

⋀ = Shoulder Seam

Color A – Natural Dk Gray 509
Color B – Natural Med Gray 508
Color C – Natural Lt Gray 507
Color D – Natural Dk Brown 501
Color E – Natural Copper 502
Color F – Natural Med Tan 503

Colors

A B C D E F

Mitered
Dmd #1
(A, E, D)

Mitered
Dmd
#2

Mitered
Dmd
#3

Mitered Dmd #1
(A, F, E)

Mitered Dmd #1
(A, E, D)

Mitered Dmds #2 & 3

Mitered Dmd #1
(A, E, C)

Mitered Dmd #1
(A, E, D)

Mitered Dmd #1
(A, F, E)

Fronts

Back

Work in this direction

Mitered Dmd #1
(A, B, C)

Mitered Dmd #1
(A, B, D)

Mitered Dmd #1
(A, B, C)

Mitered Dmd #1
(A, D, B)

Mitered Dmd #1
(A, E, D)

60" [152.4cm]

44" [111.8cm]

Layer 4 Left Edge Diamond

With A, pick up and k17 sts along the left edge of the layer 3 Left Edge Diamond, then cast on 17 sts on the same needle using whatever cast on method you prefer.

Follow the chart for Mitered Diamond #1, work with colors A, B, C.

Center Large Diamond

With A, pick up and k17 sts along the left edge of the layer 3 Right Edge Diamond, then pick up and k17 more sts along the left edge of the layer 2 Right Edge Diamond—34 sts. Pick up 1 st at top of the initial Front Diamond, then pick up and k34 sts along the right edges of the layer 2 and 3 Left Edge Diamonds—69 sts total.

Following the chart for Mitered Diamond #3, work with colors A, E, C, D, B, F, A, B, C, D, and E, working in garter st and changing colors as charted. In the color change rows, purl the center st as in all other diamonds, and work the current and new colors together using the Twisted Float Trim.

Remaining Front Diamonds

Work diamonds immediately to the left and right of the upper portion of the Center Large Diamond using the Mitered Diamond #2 chart and picking up 17 sts for each side of the diamond—34 sts before working Row 1 of chart. Work colors as charted, and work WS color change rows as for Center Large Diamond.

Work the final 3 layers of the Fronts in the same manner as the back, working 4 diamonds in the layer above the Center Large Diamond, nest 3 diamonds into the layer above that, and ending with 4 diamonds in the final layer of each Front.

Finishing

Block Back and Fronts thoroughly with steam.

Lay Back WS up and nest Fronts along top layer of Back diamonds as shown in layout on page 48. If desired, baste Fronts to Back, then with crochet hook and one of the neutral colors of remaining yarn, crochet top layers of Front diamonds to top layer of Back diamonds as shown, working in a large zigzag, leaving center top diamond on the Back unattached to the front.

Refer to the layout and turn the diamonds along the outer and center edges where marked with a dashed line. Whipstitch these diamond points to the WS of the work, creating a firm edge along the sides and front of the ruana. Steam block again.

Crochet Edging (optional)

With crochet hook and A, work 3 rows of sc along turned under edges of the ruana (sides and along center front and neckline.) Finish with 1 row of rev sc (crab st) to create a firm edge which will wear well.

Designer Bio

Annie Modesitt is author of *Confessions of a Knitting Heretic* (ModeKnit Press, 2004), the popular *Flip Knits* series (ModeKnit Press, 2007), and *Romantic Hand Knits* (Potter Craft, 2007), as well as contributing to and writing several other knitting books. Her work has appeared in *Interweave Knits*, *Vogue Knitting*, *Knitters Magazine*, *Cast On*, *Family Circle Easy Knitting*, *McCalls Needlework* and several family-oriented magazines. Annie knits using the Combination Method and believes that there truly is no wrong way to knit. She lives in St Paul, Minnesota, with her husband, kids, and assorted pets. Read more and check out her teaching schedule at her website, www.anniemodesitt.com.

South

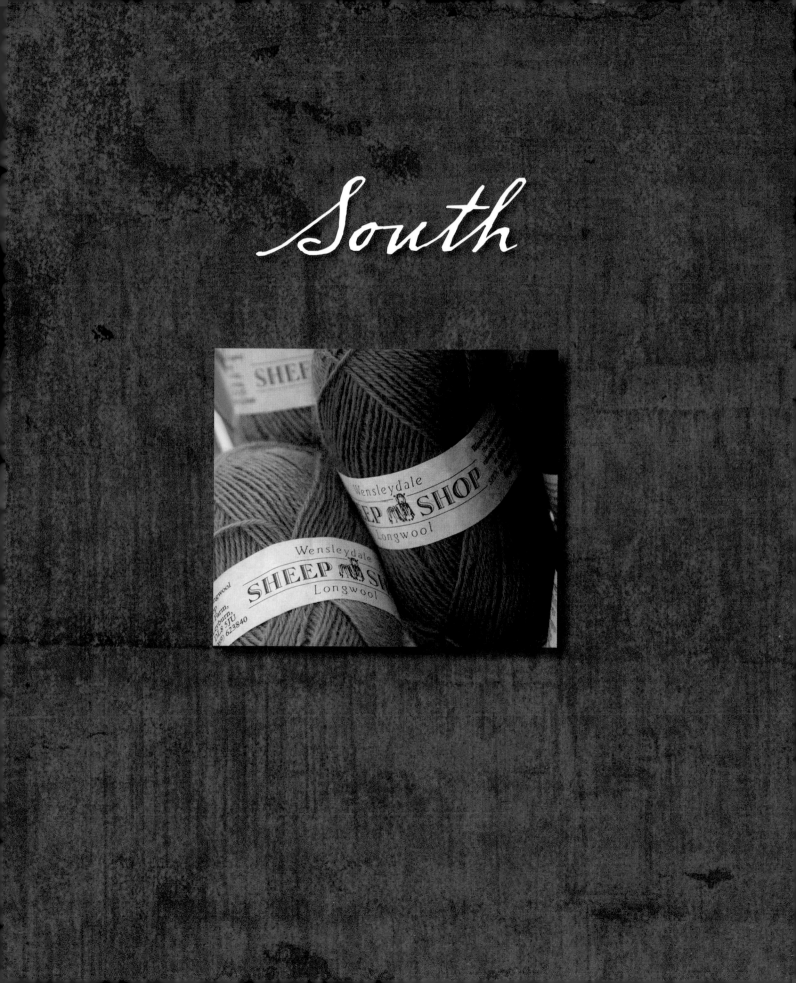

chapter 4

Southeastern Animal Fiber Fair

It's cool and the leaves are just on the verge of bursting into color along the Blue Ridge Mountains as we head to SAFF, the Southeastern Animal Fiber Fair, for the last weekend in October. For many vendors and attendees, this is the last hurrah of the festival season, the very last outing of the year. Many of the vendors attend multiple festivals and travel the country from spring to fall to sell their fibery wares. As Greg Francisco of Jehovah Jireh Farm puts it, "This is a growing market." He indicates that in their eyes, there are plenty of customers to go around. He's happy to celebrate the successes of some of his fellow fiber mill colleagues.

SAFF is well-known as a fun and ever-growing regional event in the Southeast, and people travel long distances to attend. There are warnings from friends that the parking lot at the Western North Carolina Agricultural Center might be full, and that food at the fairgrounds might be sparse. These issues are nothing when the whole scope of the festival is taken in.

Walk into the arena area, and most of the vendors are arrayed before you throughout this covered and warm location. This is important on a fall day that starts out brisk. Since the festival has grown in size, there are also vendors at an outdoor barn, using animal stalls as their "shops." The other barns and buildings hold sheep, goats, llamas, and alpacas with plenty of room to spare. The animal buildings are a quiet oasis on Friday, while the shopping areas hum with activity. Even on a weekday, the serious shoppers descend from far and wide. By Saturday at noon, the parking lot's full and every space is valued.

With approximately 7,500 people attending SAFF over three days, but with small entrance fees only on Saturday and Sunday, the numbers, and indeed, the shopping income, shows that it might be a bigger show than it appears at first glance. Lori Flood, a felter with multicolored Norwegian wool felting batts and silk for sale, says she appreciates these small but thriving venues. A well-educated crowd comes by, asking detailed questions about complicated felting techniques as I visit Lori's stall. There's a happy buzz among the shoppers, and a calm among the vendors. There's time to answer questions here, grab a cup of coffee, and enjoy the experience.

SAFF offers participants a wide array of demonstrations and classes. There are many felting, knitting, spinning, and other kinds of needlework workshops from which to choose. There are even a few workshops that have nothing to do with fiber arts, such as a chance to learn to play the harmonica. For fiber artists with more diverse interests, one can learn to build a "little" great wheel, as featured in *Spin-Off* magazine as well as how to care for camelids (alpacas, llamas, and camels) or to dye using natural dyestuffs. I walk by classes filled with serious students concentrating while they knit their first stitches, while in the next class, others learn a much more complicated technique. On one side of the arena, Lendrum spinning wheels line up in fleet formation, as students learn to spin. These beginning spinning classes are offered twice a day during the entire event, and the wheels never stop turning. The variety of learning options is

impressive, and attendees often comment on what a good value the classes are for the fees charged.

Similarly, shopping, too, spans the distance between beginning and longtime fiber artists. Pick up your first spindle or knitting needles, or order your own Weaver's Bench, Spinner's Chair, or Knitter's Rocker from Walter Turpening, who constructs the wooden frame to fit your measurements. Then, he hand weaves the cotton seat in an ergonomic design with cotton cord he braids himself.

On the other side of the sports arena I check out woodworker Lyle Wheeler's handmade great wheels, which spin like butter and have a 6-month waiting list. A crowd gathers whenever a spinner decides to try one of his masterpieces. Meanwhile, there's a constant stream of people carrying around their angora rabbits through the booths. Friends stop to pet every cuddly acquisition. Angora rabbits are common at many festivals, but at

Haleigh Anderson and her llama await competition in the show ring.

A fleet of Lendrum wheels for beginning spinners.

SAFF, many are bought, sold, and admired as a part of the activities.

For me, this is a homecoming of sorts. I see many friends from my time living in North Carolina. I feel at home, on familiar ground. However, that doesn't stop me from noticing that competition is fierce, even among friends. The SAFF participants take competition seriously, and enter their skeins; knitted, woven, and felted items; fleeces; and animals into shows to be judged. The hand-spun, hand-knitted and hand-woven pieces are pieces of art, well-designed and well-executed. When someone wins a ribbon at SAFF, your peers respect you. It's a big honor, and no one takes it for granted. This is a fine festival, worth competing in and visiting from afar. Even taking a break to sit in the stands while knitting and visiting with a friend makes for a wonderful festival experience.

Asheville

Asheville is well-known for its arts and crafts tradition. Any visitor to the area would be missing something if she didn't drive down the highway 20 minutes to downtown Asheville. While at SAFF, Marie Hendricks, co-owner of Asheville NC Homecrafts, makes sure to invite me personally to visit her shop at the Historic Grove Arcade in the middle of Asheville. I meet her partner, Judy, as she straightens the traditional baskets in the stall, which she makes herself. Everything Marie says about the downtown shop, in its lovely restored building, and the size and success of her enterprise is absolutely true. Drawing on the strong historic tradition of Southern Appalachian women, who beautified their homes and used scarce resources to enrich their lives, Asheville NC Homecrafts features hand-spun yarns, hand-knit hats and scarves, quilts, and other items all made from scratch in a 100-mile radius of the shop. As well, you can find knitting yarns and other goodies right there, amongst the art galleries and other boutiques that fill the Arcade.

Fiber arts don't end there. This area features weavers as artists in residence at some of its galleries, and spinning and weaving appear frequently in town. Asheville, filled with funky handmade art, good food, and high-end shopping, is worth a visit, especially if you've got a yen to see true fiber art before or after SAFF takes place.

Quick Felted Sweater Bag

Need to make a bag fast to take to the festival to carry all your loot? No time to knit one? Recycle a wool sweater and sew one together quickly! The bag is flexible enough to stuff with lots of yarn and fiber but also very sturdy.

Designed by Cindy Moore

Skill level

Intermediate

Finished Measurements

Approx 16 × 12" (40.6 x 30.5cm)

Note Exact size will be determined by the size of the sweater you select and the felting process.

Materials

- Men's XL or larger V neck 100 percent wool sweater

  Note While these instructions suggest a V neck, any style of sweater will make a great felted bag.

- Top loading washing machine
- Small amount of detergent
- Zippered pillow case cover and safety pin
- Large towel or old jeans
- Scissors or rotary cutter
- Purchased straps with metal rings at ends (or straps from an old bag)
- Sewing thread
- Fabric glue or hot glue
- Sewing machine
- 4" (10cm) Velcro hook and loop tape, ½" (1.25 cm) wide
- Straight pins

Instructions

Felting the Sweater

1. Using the lowest water level setting, fill the top-loading washing machine with the hottest water available. Add a small amount of detergent. If you use no-rinse wool-wash soap, you will not have to rinse the sweater.

2. Put your sweater into a zippered pillow case cover and secure the zipper with a safety pin so it doesn't open during the wash cycle. Put the bagged sweater into the washer with a large bath towel or a couple of pairs of old jeans.

3. Allow the washer to go through the wash cycle, but do not allow it to spin. Spinning a felted item can cause permanent creases that will not come out. Check about every 5 to 10 minutes to see if the sweater has felted.

4. Continue the agitation until the sweater has felted to the desired size or until you can no longer see the stitches. The longer you felt the sweater, the stronger the fabric will be and the smaller the bag will be.

5. Dry flat.

Making the Bag

Cutting the Felted Sweater

1. Cut the sleeves off of the felted sweater. Make sure to cut off the seams with the sleeves.

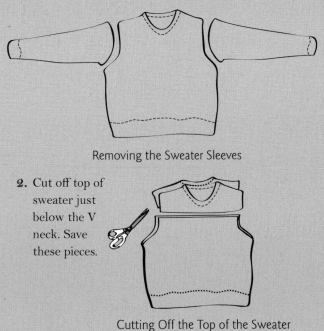

Removing the Sweater Sleeves

2. Cut off top of sweater just below the V neck. Save these pieces.

Cutting Off the Top of the Sweater

Sewing the Bag

3. Turn the sweater inside out, so the WS is facing out. Using the sewing machine, sew across both layers at the top of the sweater where the V neck was removed, stitching on the WS. This creates the bottom of the bag and will be referred to as the bottom seam.

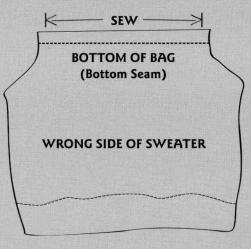

Sewing Across the Top of the Sweater

4. Fold the original armholes together and pin. Repeat for the other side of sweater. Sew along pinned edges.

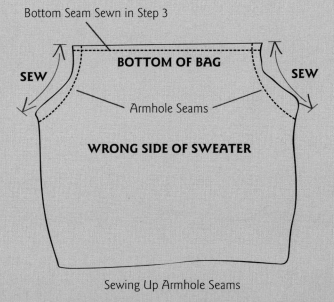

Sewing Up Armhole Seams

5. Snip corners.

Snipped Corner

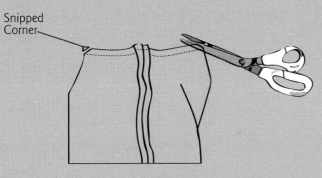

Snipping Corners

Finishing

Attaching the Straps

6. Turn the bag right side out.

7. Cut the front V-neck ribbing from sweater as close to the seam as possible, then cut the ribbing in half.

Note *You can use the sleeve cuffs if you do not have a V-neck sweater or if your sweater has no neck ribbing.*

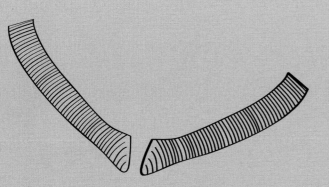

Cutting V-Neck Ribbing in Half

8. Slip one of the V-neck ribbing pieces through the 2 metal loops on 1 end of the strap. Fold ribbing and sew it to the inside of sweater bag on top of the side seam, reinforcing the seam by sewing over it several times. Repeat with the other 2 strap ends on the other side of the sweater bag.

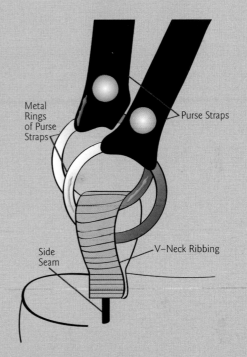

Metal Rings of Purse Straps

Purse Straps

Side Seam

V–Neck Ribbing

Attaching V–Neck Ribbing to Bag

Flap

9. Fold the top of sweater back in half along the neck edge. Cut from the neck edge to the bottom edge. You can remove the tags or leave them in.

10. To make the bag flap, pin the bottom edge of the top of the sweater to the top of the bag. Center the flap between the side seams. Sew the pinned edge to the top of the bag.

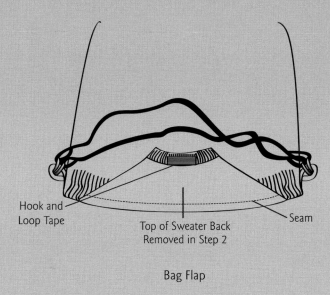

Hook and Loop Tape

Top of Sweater Back Removed in Step 2

Seam

Bag Flap

FOLD

Top of Sweater Back Removed in Step 2

Shaping Bag Flap from Top of Sweater

11. Cut the rough side of a piece of Velcro hook and loop tape about 4" (10 cm) long. Glue it to the bag flap with fabric glue or hot glue. The Velcro hook and loop tape will easily stick to the wool.

12. Turn the bag upside down, close the flap, throw the straps over your shoulder, and you're ready to go!

Designer Bio

Cindy Moore is a knitter, seamstress, artist, illustrator, editor, graphic designer, and fitness expert. Creating and designing felted bags from recycled sweaters has become one of her passions. Read more about Cindy Moore at her Web site: www.technicalillustrator.net/FitterKnitter.html.

Blossom

This lace scarf is the perfect accessory for casual or dress wear, day or evening. The pattern features a simple edging which is attached while it is knit. The custom colorway and simple lace pattern perfectly complement each other for a decidedly feminine but urban feel. Brooks Farm, a vendor with an online presence and a stall at many of the festivals, has created a new hand-dyed yarn in a colorway especially for this pattern.

Designed by JoLene Treace

Skill level

Intermediate

Finished Measurements

60 × 8" (152.4 × 20.3cm), blocked (see gauge note on page 60)

Materials

- Approximately 500 yd. (457m) of lace weight or fingering weight yarn that knits up at the appropriate gauge

Sample knit with: Brooks Farm *Acero* (60 percent superwash wool, 20 percent silk, 20 percent viscose; 420 yd. [384m] per 4 oz. [113g] skein; approx 7.5 wraps per inch): color Blossom, 2 skeins

Other swatches pictured on page 62 were knit with: Knitting Notions *Classic Merino Lace* (100 percent Merino, 388 yd. [355m] per 1.75 oz. [50g] skein; approx 9 wraps per inch): color Tea Rose, 2 skeins and Blackberry Ridge *Silky Merino* (50 percent silk, 50 percent Merino; 600 yd. [548.6m] per 2 oz. [57g] skein; approx 10 wraps per inch): color Pink, 1 skein.

Note   Many spinners measure the thickness of yarn in wraps per inch. Lace weight varies enormously in terms of wraps per inch and grist (thickness or diameter of yarn) compared to other yarn weights. The 2 additional swatches shown illustrate how different the lace looks with different yarn—both fingering weight and lace weight. The photo that shows several swatches gives discerning knitters and spinners something to aim for, which is important in a yarn that is hard to get except at festivals or online.

- US size 3 (3.25mm) circular needle, 32" (81.3cm) long and 1 double pointed needle of same size, *or size needed for desired effect of dressed laciness of fabric*
- Tapestry needle
- Blocking board (optional) and blocking wires or rust-proof pins

Gauge

When measuring a blocked lace swatch:

20 sts = 4" (10cm) with Brooks Farm *Acero*

22 sts = 4" (10cm) with Knitting Notions *Classic Merino Lace*

24 sts = 4" (10cm) with Blackberry Ridge *Silky Merino*

Note Gauge is somewhat flexible with lace knitting especially for a scarf, which does not require a precise fit. Each scarf will block to a slightly different size, but all will be beautiful. Row gauge is not critical and will vary depending on how the piece is blocked.

Pattern Stitches

Blossom Stitch

Worked over a multiple of 8 + 11.

Slip all sts purlwise.

Row 1 (RS): Sl1, k1, YO, ssk, k2, *k1, k2tog, YO, k1, YO, ssk, k2; rep from * to last 5 sts, k1, k2tog, YO, k2.

Row 2 (and all WS rows): Sl1, purl to end.

Row 3: Sl1, k2, YO, ssk, k1, *k2tog, YO, k3, YO, ssk, k1; rep from * to last 5 sts, k2tog, YO, k3.

Row 5: Sl1, k1, k2tog, YO, k2, *k1, YO, ssk, k1, k2tog, YO, k2; rep from * to last 5 sts, k1, YO, ssk, k2.

Row 7: Sl1, k2tog, YO, k3, *k2, YO, sl1, k2tog, psso, YO, k3; rep from * to last 5 sts, k2, YO, ssk, k1.

Row 9: Sl1, k2, k2tog, YO, k1, *YO, ssk, k3, k2tog, YO, k1; rep from * to last 5 sts, YO, ssk, k3.

Row 11: Sl1, k1, k2tog, YO, k2, *k1, YO, ssk, k1, k2tog, YO, k2; rep from * to last 5 sts, k1, YO, ssk, k2.

Row 13: Sl1, k2, YO, ssk, k1, *k2tog, YO, k3, YO, ssk, k1; rep from * to last 5 sts, k2tog, YO, k3.

Row 15: Sl1, k3, YO, sl1, k2tog, psso, *YO, k5, YO, sl1, k2tog, psso; rep from * to last 4 sts, YO, k4.

Repeat rows 1–16 for patt.

Side Edging

Begins with 5 sts, increases to 10 sts, and decreases back to 5 sts.

Slip all sts purlwise.

Row 1 (RS): Sl1, k2, YO, k2.

Row 2, 4, 6, 8 and 10 (WS): Sl1, knit to last st, k2tog (joining last st on edging and next st on scarf).

Row 3: Sl1, k3, YO, k2.

Row 5: Sl1, k4, YO, k2.

Row 7: Sl1, k5, YO, k2.

Row 9: Sl1, k6, YO, k2.

Row 11: Sl1, k9.

Row 12: BO 5, k to last st, k2tog (joining last st on edging and next st on scarf).

Repeat rows 1–12 for patt.

Top and Bottom Edging

Begins with 5 sts, increases to 10 sts, and decreases back to 5 sts.

Slip all sts purlwise.

Row 1 (RS): Sl1, k2, YO, k2.

Row 2 and 8 (WS): Sl1, knit to last st, sl1, k2tog, psso (joining last st on edging and next 2 sts on scarf).

Row 3: Sl1, k3, YO, k2.

Rows 4, 6 and 10: Sl1, knit to last st, k2tog (joining last st on edging and next st on scarf).

Row 5: Sl1, k4, YO, k2.

Row 7: Sl1, k5, YO, k2.

Row 9: Sl1, k6, YO, k2.

Row 11: Sl1, k9.

Row 12: BO 5, k to last st, k2tog (joining last st on edging and next st on scarf).

Repeat rows 1–12 for patt.

Blossom Stitch

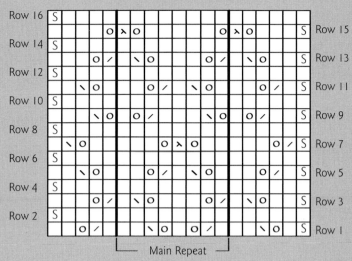

Main Repeat

Key

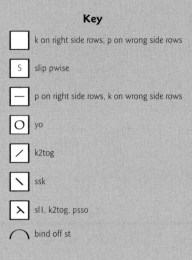

	k on right side rows, p on wrong side rows
S	slip pwise
—	p on right side rows, k on wrong side rows
O	yo
/	k2tog
\	ssk
⅄	sl1, k2tog, psso
⌒	bind off st

Side Edging

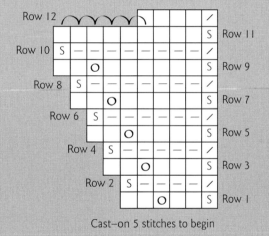

Cast–on 5 stitches to begin

Top and Bottom Edging

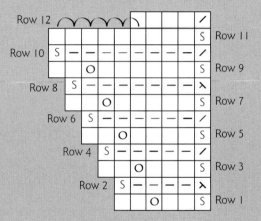

Instructions

Note *You will be working a chained slipstitch selvage at the sides of the scarf (included in line by line directions and charts for scarf and edging). Knitting progresses from the bottom edge (cast on edge) to the top edge of the scarf. When length is complete, you will pick up and knit stitches along the entire circumference of the scarf. At this point, all the stitches are on hold on the circular needle and will be bound off in a decrease as the edging is worked and attached.*

Scarf

Cast on 35 sts with Russian lace cast-on as follows:

Hold 2 knitting needles together and work long tail cast-on over both needles, taking care not to crowd the stitches. After sts are cast on, pull second needle out of cast-on sts. You will have a loop at the base of each stitch that may be picked up and knitted into when working the set up round for the edging.

Work in Blossom Stitch until 22 repeats have been completed, ending after row 16 of patt.

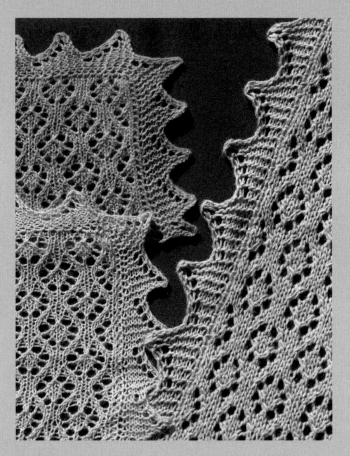

Note If you decide to adjust the length of the scarf, you must add or subtract repeats in multiples of 2 for the edging to come out evenly.

Edging Set Up

Next row (RS): K2tog, knit to last 2 sts, ssk, place marker—33 sts rem, 176 chained loops along the side of the scarf.

Pick up and knit 180 sts on long end of scarf as follows: Pick up and knit 2 sts in each of the first 2 selvage chains by inserting the needle underneath the first loop of the chain and knitting 1 st, then underneath both loops of the same selvage chain and knitting an additional st. Pick up and knit 1 st for each remaining selvage chain up to last 2 selvage chains, and work these as you did the first 2. Place marker.

Pick up and knit 33 sts along cast-on edge as follows: Pick up and knit into the loops at base of the cast-on sts. Place marker.

Work remaining long side as you did the first—426 sts total, 33 sts on each short end and 180 sts on each long edge.

Turn the work as you normally would when not working in the round. Cast on 5 sts.

Edging

Note Odd rows are worked away from the scarf, towards the outside of the edging. Even rows are worked away from the edging, towards the scarf, and are the rows that the edging is attached.

Using the dpn to knit the edging, begin with the side of the scarf by knitting across the edging cast-on stitches up to the last edging stitch. To attach the edging, k2tog (the last edging st and first scarf st on the left needle).

Work rows 1–12 of Side Edging patt until you will have completed 30 points (or repeats, as the edging forms 1 point for each repeat) along the side of the scarf.

You are now ready to continue the edging along the bottom of the scarf. Remove marker, and work rows 1–12 of Top and Bottom Edging patt across the bottom edge of the scarf, working sl1, k2tog, psso instead of k2tog at the end of the last repeat.

Remove marker, and work the remaining side as the first, then the top as you did the bottom.

BO rem 5 sts and break yarn, leaving a 6" (15.2cm) tail. Thread tapestry needle with tail, and sew the CO and BO edges together with an overcast stitch.

Finishing

Block scarf to dimensions or as desired, leaving pinned for at least 24 hours to dry and set.

Designer Bio

JoLene Treace is a designer from the Midwest. She delights in bringing her personal inspirations into her designs, so that each of her designs has a story to tell. She has designs published in books and magazines, as well as a line of pattern leaflets. A list of vendors and wholesale distributors is available on her website, as well as a link to her blog where she discusses the business and process of knitting design. Her Web site is www.atimetoknit.com.

chapter 5

The Tennessee State Fair

A Spinning Competition and Fleece Auction

Pay your state fair admission fee, walk up the midway, and it feels like you're miles away from the fiber arts world. The flashing lights and bells of the games draw you in . . . but there's always something much more alluring ahead at the Tennessee State Fair, held every year in September in Nashville. A quilter, knitter, or fiber artist of any kind might be drawn to the Creative Arts building, to see the ribbons on the best entries, and of course, in Music City, live music of all kinds pulls in the passersby. Hear the gospel performance and at the next stage, you'll be slowed by a jazz big band, a famous country musician, or the percussive Kenyan acrobats. The scent of popcorn, funnel cake, and other fair delights causes irrational hunger. Gosh knows why, but suddenly a fried Oreo sounds like a good idea.

Throughout the week, you can see the spinning demonstrations at the "Volunteer Village" or the new ongoing sheep-to-shawl competition, but on one particular weekday night during the week-long Tennessee State Fair, handspinners from all over Tennessee and even parts of Kentucky converge on the Vaughn Building. Inside, miles of sheep—sheep raised mainly for their meat, not their wool—are housed in temporary pens under florescent lights. The midway, music and food disappear in a chorus of baas and bleats. The blur of large fans and sheep bedding fill the air with the aroma of sheep. Most of the people in the building this evening are here for the sheep competitions. They line up in front of the judge, showing off their ewes and rams, hoping to win prize money for the best of show in categories based on breed (Dorset, Suffolk, and Hampshire) or "Champion Tennessee Ram."

Spinners might be distracted by a sheep's pretty face, but off to the corner, the siren song of the spinning competitions and fleece auction calls. From Black Welsh Mountain and Border Cheviot to Shropshire and Southdown, the fleeces are lined up along the walls. There are also categories for "Commercial" and "White hand spinning" fleeces, both ewe and ram. This allows for those beautiful mixed-breed fleeces that sometimes defy description.

Every year, this competition grows. Organized by Tennessee State Fair Department Head Kim Caulfield of *Far Out Farm*, the show in 2007 had approximately 230 fleeces entered, making it one of the biggest fleece shows (if not the biggest) in the South. The fleeces are judged by well-known experts in the field. In 2006, Susan McFarland of Susan's Fiber Shop in Wisconsin flew into Nashville in order to judge the event. In 2007, LeRoy Johnson from Wyoming did the honors. Morris Culver, another luminary in the shepherding world, judged a few years ago. Shepherds enter their fleeces for the premiums, which can amount to big money per fleece—first place in any of the categories is $22 per fleece, more than the shepherds will generally earn for any of the individual fleeces when sold commercially at the local wool pool.

Before the fleece auction begins, a congenial spinning competition takes place, also run by Kim Caulfield and her mother Jane. The premise is simple. Everyone gets the same amount of beautifully prepared roving from Kim's Romney flock. Who can spin the longest single ply yarn in 10 minutes? There are two categories for both spindle and spinning wheel competitions. Each category has both a "beginner class," and an "open class" for more experienced spinners. Competition is informal, but individuals can be fierce in their pursuit of first place.

This might be partly due to the prizes. There are small monetary awards for these events, almost enough to reimburse your gas money and entrance to the fair, but the real treats are selected by Kim, who carefully solicits prizes sure to tempt spinners. One year, there might be camel roving, another year, she might find super-fine Merino, yak, high quality spindles, hand-dyed roving, or wool combs for the prize winners. Each year, Kim's carefully selected special prizes are the major draw, besides knowing that you're the "fastest spinner in Tennessee."

Sheep wear coats so they are clean for the show ring.

Just a few of the fleeces on display.

Crowds gather to watch the spinning and to listen to the witty exchanges. Lots of laughing and shrieks accompany the event, as well as cries of "How much more time?" and "Oh, the pressure!"

Finally, the contestants count their hand-spun yardage and the winners are announced. The crowds of spectators disperse, and the spinners settle down to the serious business of choosing fleeces. Cotswolds, Jacobs, Shetlands, and the mixed breed handspinning fleeces are popular, as well as the special categories of prepared roving. Rarely does the auction end up in a bidding war. Most of the time, the buyer consults the shepherd's minimum price, writes a check to the shepherd, and leaves with a gorgeous, prize-winning fleece. Shepherds who enter fleeces at the fair often aim for the ribbons and don't ask much for their fleeces. Savvy spinners are thrilled by their bargains. Kim

Caulfield encourages spinners to write notes to the shepherds and report back to them about what they liked about the fleece they purchased.

The evening winds down, spinning wheels are packed up and spinners disperse into the night, carrying huge plastic bags full of award-winning raw fleece along with their wheels. Even when spinners buy multiple fleeces, the fleece show looks full when we leave. On the way out of the fairgrounds, late night BMX racing displays compete with rides that light up the sky. On the bandstand, three guys in cowboy hats and boots sing Steve Miller's "The Joker," and the crowd sings along.

For this spinner, it's 70 miles of highway driving to get home, but the gathering is so much fun that it is worth the trip, year after year. I might just be washing the first fleece late tonight, before I fall asleep.

How to Wash Fleece: A General Guide

Want to buy a raw fleece, fresh from the shearing floor, but you're not sure how to clean it yourself? Here are instructions to help you through the process. Every fiber artist will fine tune this, so see this as a step-by-step way to get started. This is by no means my invention! It's simply a combination of things I've found to work. I invite you to experiment, as many generations of wool workers have done before us.

The most important aspect of this process is to avoid felting the wool. Felt is a fabric of wool (or any combination of fiber) that is worked together by pressure and agitation. This is an irreversible process. Felt is a useful fabric, but you can't spin the fiber if it's felted. While getting the wool clean is a goal, as long as you don't felt the wool, you can start again and continue washing until it gets clean.

Here are two methods. The first is a basic method in which anyone can wash a small amount of fleece without any equipment at all. This is probably the way most of the world once washed or still washes fleece. The second method is the "deluxe" method. There's no need to use all this equipment but you can wash a lot of fleece in an efficient manner with the deluxe approach. In either case, the most important part of this process is to avoid any kind of wringing or agitation, because this makes felt.

Basic Washing

Materials

- A fleece (if not already skirted, please see p. 98)
- Source of hot water
- Clean container or sink
- Liquid dish soap (optional: biodegradable detergent)

  Note If you use a biodegradable detergent, you can reuse your brown water on your garden or lawn. It's a form of manure tea that's very popular among organic farmers worldwide!

- A sunny day
- Clean outdoor surface or an old bed sheet
- Washing machine, mesh onion bag, lingerie bag, or salad spinner (optional)

Instructions

1. Take hot water that is just cool enough to immerse your hands in and put it in your clean container.

2. Add a liberal amount of dish soap.

3. If you have a mesh bag, put your fleece in it, then immerse your fleece in the water. If you don't have a mesh bag, just immerse the fleece. It takes a moment for the fleece to absorb the water, because the lanolin in fleece is water resistant—this is what keeps sheep dry out in their pastures. As soon as the fleece is wet—you may help this with your hands but do not squish the fleece—the water will be brown.

4. Gently take out the fleece with your hands and dump out this water.

5. Fill up your container with hot rinse water.

6. Continue to rinse, dump out the water, take out the fleece, and repeat until the water runs clear. The brown residue is lanolin, suint (sheep sweat) and all the dirt, manure, and nature that the sheep has encountered since its last shearing. Generally, the water runs clear after 2 or 3 rinses. If the water is

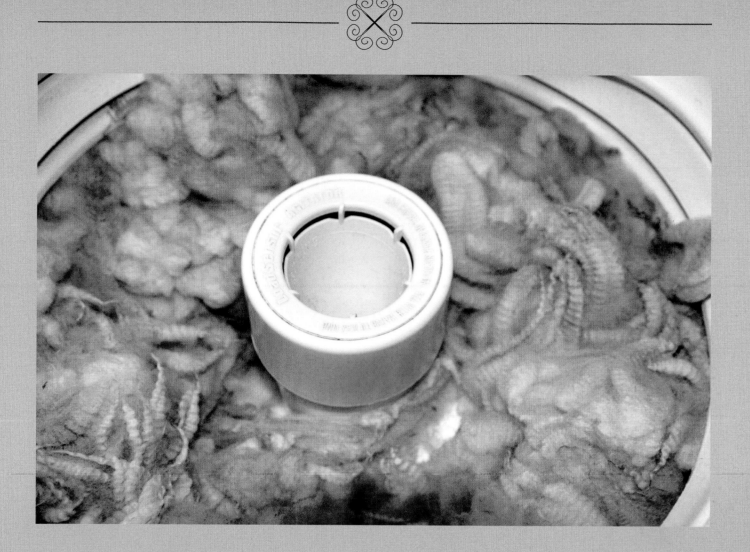

still dirty after 3 hot water rinses, make another hot, soapy mixture and repeat from #3.

Note *Avoid running hot water on top of your fleece because this can felt the wool immediately! Instead, take the fleece out of the water and re-immerse it in fresh hot water each time.*

Drying Fleece

1. When you feel the wool is clean enough, (*enough* is the key word here—this varies greatly from spinner to spinner) you have several options:

   The lowest tech option is to take the dripping wet wool, place it on a clean surface outside, and leave it there to dry. This works well in a place with low humidity. In humid parts of the world, you'll wait a long time for that wool to dry. Also, there is a likelihood of mold growing or birds using the wool for nests by the time it has dried. (Both of these things have happened to me in the southeastern United States.)

   The next option is to take the wool in the mesh bag outside. Then, swing the wool above your head in a circular motion as fast as you can without getting dizzy and falling down. This is called *wuzzing*, and is actually an ancient way to dry wool. Alternate the spinning with banging the wool on a hard surface that you don't mind getting wet. (The side of your house works.) Also, this is great for getting out any aggressions you might have! When you get tired, lay the wool out to dry in the sun on a clean surface or an old sheet on the ground. The wool will dry much faster now that you've taken out some of the excess water.

   If you aren't up to wuzzing, use a salad spinner to spin out the wool, just as you would spin the water from your lettuce.

The highest technology option works the best, but there is more risk of felting involved. Using your washing machine, figure out how to set it so you are just using the spin cycle, which will get the water out of the fleece. (Most top loading washers allow for this, but washers vary.) Avoid any agitation or water! The spin cycle is usually at the very end of your washer's cycle. The first time I use a new washer, I run it with nothing inside to be sure it is just spinning water out, and nothing else. Put the clean, wet fleece in the washer on the spin cycle. When the washer finishes spinning the water out, put the wool outside to dry.

2. Make absolutely sure the wool has dried for a long time before putting it away in a bag or sack. Bring the wool in at the end of the sunny day. Don't leave it out overnight, because it will get wet with dew and you'll have to start all over again getting it dry. When the wool is inside, leave it out for a day inside, and then put it away. Wool can hold a lot of water in it and still feel dry. This can then result in a stinky mold effect when you package it up and put it away.

Storing Fleece

The best fleece storage container is an old pillow case or sheet, or a cardboard or paper bag. This will allow the fleece to "breathe." In a plastic bag, humidity changes and damp can cause a fleece to rot. If you want to store fleece for a long time, it will attract fewer moths if it is clean. Raw fleece is especially tempting, not just for moths, but also for dogs and cats, who are attracted by the odor and can become ill if they ingest wool.

Deluxe Washing

Materials

- Top loading washing machine or one that easily allows for manual stopping and starting (see below)

- Liquid detergent (I use a "free-and-clear" variety, but you can use anything—people argue about this one)

- A lot of fleece (up to 4 or 5 lbs [1.8–2.3k] will fit in a family sized washer, but you can wash less in the machine)

- Paper towels to wipe out the washer when you are finished

- A clean old bedsheet or window screens or an old screen door

- Bricks or something else to prop up the screens on outside

- A sunny day, an unused room with good airflow, or a wood stove

- Bleach to clean out your washer (optional)

- Borax OR rubbing alcohol, OR vinegar to add to the rinse water if you have hard water (you'll know if you do—nothing else gets clean easily in hard water, either) (optional)

Instructions

1. Fill up the washer with your regular amount of detergent for 1 load (2 loads if this is a **really** dirty fleece) and hot water. Do **not** add bleach; it will ruin your fleece.

2. Shut off your washing machine so that you have a full tub of standing hot water.

3. Immerse the fleece gently into the water. Leave the fleece in the hot water until the water begins to cool and the fleece is entirely immersed. This wait can be anywhere from 15 minutes to a few hours, based on the kind of fleece, the heat of the water, and the business of your day.

4. Use the spin cycle only to get that dirty water out of your fleece.

5. Take the dripping fleece out if it is a breed that is prone to felting. (Always do this with a fine wool or Merino fleece.) Refill the tub with hot rinse water. If it is a breed not prone to felting (see the book *In Sheep's Clothing* by Jane and Nola Fournier [*Interweave Press*, 2003] for an expert opinion on how common sheep breeds felt), you can refill the tub with hot water while leaving the fleece in the washer. Do not let the machine agitate at any time! Know your washer's cycles.

6. Use the spin cycle to get the dirty rinse water out and repeat with a second hot rinse.

7. If the fleece looks clean at this point, take it out of the washing machine and set it up on those window screens. Make sure the screen is propped up off of the ground to promote good airflow. In case of rainstorms, freezing temperatures, or big winds, don't put fleece outside. Find a good place indoors—near a wood stove, in an unused room with good circulation, or, in my case, a corner of the dining room, near a heating vent.

8. Repeat this washing process if your fleece still doesn't look clean. If your fleece still contains lanolin, dirt, and suint at this point, it's best to repeat this process now instead of letting it dry and starting again. You can always rewash a fleece after it has dried but you may increase your chances of felting it.

9. For the sake of cleanliness, run your washing machine through 1 cycle without anything in it, using hot water and bleach before washing your clothing in it again. This is just to be sure that none of that "sheep stuff" ends up on your clothing or stuck in your plumbing.

Refer to "Drying Fleece" and "Storing Fleece" under "Basic Washing," found earlier in this chapter.

Some Final Notes

This washing process just looks complicated because it's written down. It's exactly like the hand-washing process you might use to wash a pair of wool socks or a sweater, and people have been doing this for thousands of years. The worst thing that could happen is for you to end up with a lot of felt. Felted fleece is ideal for:

- Dog or cat bed stuffing
- Cushion/pillow stuffing
- Mattress covers for invalids
- Mulch

Don't despair over any quirky or stinky part of this process! It comforts me to know that whatever mistakes I've made while dealing with wool, it's certain that somewhere, sometime, a person has done this before me. We've been wearing wool garments for thousands of years. All sheep are still shorn by hand and now you've learned how to wash fleece by hand, too!

Spinning for Speed

Spinning is meditative, fun, and relaxing. This project is for spinners seeking to improve their skills, so if you're a beginner, see Chapter 6's "Inexpensive Tools for Spinning" p. 79 for how to make your own inexpensive spindle and learn the basics. Yet, when you want to win a contest, finish up yarn for a big project, or spin for sale, it should also be fast. Here is a quick summary of tips to speed up your spinning. For a fabulous, in-depth look at spinning for speed and softness, be sure to read Paula Simmons' book, Spinning for Softness & Speed *(Madrona Pub., 1982).*

Wanda Shotwell competes under the bright lights.

Skill level
Intermediate

Size
One size fits all spinners!

Materials

- Spindle or spinning wheel
- Well-prepared wool roving or washed fleece
- Hand cards or drum carder
- Niddy-noddy, swift, or use of an arm as a skein winder (see Creating a Skein on page 82 for more information)
- Timer (optional)
- Ball winder (optional)
- Handy Andy (optional)
- *Spinning for Softness & Speed* by Paula Simmons (optional)

Instructions

Note All spinners can create very smooth and even yarns with practice, even while spinning quickly. In the beginning, try not to focus on evenness while learning to spin fast. Instead, focus on speed. An even yarn will follow in time, if that is your goal.

1. Begin with your fiber. To spin quickly, your fiber will need to be well-prepared. It's best to use a carded preparation (woolen) rather than a combed preparation (worsted) for this technique. This means that if you're starting with roving, pre-draft it (pull it apart) to make it lofty and easy to spin to the yarn weight you'd like to produce. If carding, be sure to create light, lofty batts or rolags. Do not overload your carder with fiber, but create airy clouds of fiber.

2. Use fast equipment. If using a spindle, choose one that is a long, fast spinner. Most people find top-whorl spindles easier to twirl more quickly, which is essential for spinning fast. If using a wheel, adjust your wheel so it pulls in the yarn onto the bobbin quickly. Choose a ratio that will introduce enough twist so you will only treadle a few times before feeding the yarn onto the bobbin. Bear in mind that wheels differ. You may have to treadle your wheel or twirl your spindle like the dickens to make this work. Some wheels and spindles are just not made for production (fast) spinning.

3. Your hand movements are important here. Most spinners seem to start out by using inchworm movements, using both hands close together near the orifice of their spinning wheels. This is a very slow way to spin. There are many ways to use your hands to

spin. The fastest method is best described in detail in *Spinning for Softness and Speed.* To improve speed for any spinner, learn the long-draw technique. In brief, the long-draw technique requires you to use your drafting hand to draft while pulling that hand back from the wheel anywhere from several inches to 2 feet. Treadle and adjust twist or drafting with the other hand if necessary, and then allow the yarn to feed on to the bobbin or spindle. A good intermediary step for this is to learn to spin one-handed. Those with great wheels, charka, or supported spindle experience will know this technique right away.

4. To spin one-handed, hold the fiber cradled in your palm, with your hand either palm up or thumb up. With a quick movement, pull back, drafting your yarn in one arm's length. Introduce twist into that length, and wind on. Use your second hand only when absolutely necessary to briefly control twist, fiber slippage, or lumps in the fiber. While most who spin on a great wheel or charka use the left hand for one-handed spinning, either hand works with a spindle or parlor wheel.

5. To increase speed, cut down on extraneous movements. Have all your fiber processed and ready, in easy arm's reach from your spinning. If using a spinning wheel, consider the use of a Woolee Winder (a level winding device available for many modern wheels) so you do not have to change hooks on your flyer to fill the bobbin. If spindling, stand up and raise your hands above your head to produce more yardage with each length spun. By the way, this is a great way to increase shoulder mobility, but if it hurts, stop! (Speed isn't everything!)

6. The only way to know if you've increased your speed is to time yourself. Set a timer for 10 minutes and begin with a just a leader on an empty bobbin or spindle. At the end of 10 minutes, skein your yarn and count up your yardage. Use this as a measure as you increase speed. Compete against yourself!

7. Another saving device is a ball winder. It's useful both for creating a center pull ball for plying and for vastly increasing your ball winding speed. If you like the meditative speed of winding balls by hand, consider using a nostepinne (a low-tech tool used for winding a center-pull ball) or Handy Andy (see Chapter 12 for more information) for increased plying speed.

Finishing Your Yarn

Set your yarn's twist as you usually would, with washing or steaming. To set twist by washing, immerse your yarn in hot water and a little bit of liquid dish soap. Rinse twice, in two more hot water baths. Squeeze out the yarn, taking care not to agitate it too much. If it's available, spin out your yarn in the spin cycle of your washer or with a salad spinner. Hang the skein up to dry. Some spinners set twist by steaming. A common technique is to carefully move the skein through the steam from a tea kettle. Use caution if you prefer this technique. Washing is generally safer. When dry, analyze your yarn for its overall twist and appearance to decide its best use. As you improve in terms of speed, make sure to see if anything else about your yarn quality suffers. It's best to have a balance between quality and speed. As you improve your skills, you can have both. In the meanwhile, be sure to alternate balls of hand-spun for each row while knitting, crocheting, or weaving in order to produce a more uniform end product.

Midwest

grown, spun &
dyed in
Michigan

chapter 6

Michigan
Fiber Festival

At first, it may be hard to imagine summoning up enthusiasm for a fiber festival in August. One calls this summer month the "dog days" for a reason. Hot and steamy weather can make it impossible to consider an event that focuses on raising sheep or spinning, knitting, and weaving with wool. Yet, all this disinterest evaporates with the hot air when one drives towards Lake Michigan and the Michigan Fiber Festival.

Michigan's cool August weather is an interesting reminder that in *some places*, people can wear sweaters in the summer time. Those people, who have much colder winters for which to prepare, are ready for their summer-time festival.

Allegan County Fairgrounds are off the beaten track, in a relatively rural setting, but still close to the Lake Michigan resorts and bigger cities such as Kalamazoo. Along the way to the festival, signs for U-Pick peaches, blueberries, and raspberries abound. The land is verdant, dark, and lush. It's easy to understand why so many fiber animals grow lovely fleeces in Michigan's cool and damp climate.

The festival has plenty of room at the fairgrounds for animal displays, 100 vendors, and 8,000 to 10,000 weekend visitors. Run by volunteers, there's always someone nearby to answer questions or smile at attendees. The festival, in its 10th year, has the usual array of classes, as well as competitions for best fleeces, skeins, and garments. The animals on show include a variety of sheep, Angora rabbits, alpacas, Angora goats, and even a sheep dog demonstration.

After seeing a serious sheep dog trial or two and a very polished demonstration at other events, I wonder how the average farmer and dog manage things. The Curts family of Crowded Byre Farm in Ladoga, Indiana, does the herding demonstration every year. They focus on breeding, training, and raising border collies for farmers. When I spoke with Jackie Curts, she explained that there are perhaps 12 to 15 breeding ewes and some cattle with which the dogs practice. They also have 12 dogs, as well as a preschooler named Duncan and an infant. While the usual herding demonstration interests onlookers, as soon as the sheep are penned, the real excitement begins. All seven dogs at the event, released from their crates, rush into the fenced enclosure. Duncan wrestles and plays with his dogs. Multiple dogs visit the crowds, wagging and licking those who watched the herding demonstration. All at once, you can see that Michigan Fiber Festival is a relaxed affair for this whole family!

In the children's activity area, piles of multicolored yarns are heaped on a table. At least 10 kids bend seriously over their *kumihimo*, a Japanese braiding project. While parents watch, these kids make their own corded bracelets, necklaces, and key chains, using inexpensive stiff foam circles with notches for their *marudai*, or kumihimo braiding tool. Meanwhile, in another vendor's tent, I meet the Alpaca Barber, Dave Binkowski, and his family. Dave shears approximately 1,300 alpaca each year, during a 90-day shearing period, with the help of his daughters. When he's not shearing, Dave focuses on making small braiding and weaving tools and creates small wooden tabletop marudai, inkle looms, and lucets. Each one is different, hand done from a one of a kind piece of wood. Dave is beloved by many in the Michigan alpaca breeders' community; they're just sorry he can't fit in more visits to their farms to shear.

Harmony and Grits, a Michigan-based Roots music duo, fills the air as we visit many vendors. Felted batts, contemporary ceramic buttons, and every color of hand-dyed fiber and yarn adorn the booths. I'm constantly stopping to touch and admire things which catch my eye. Especially alluring are signs that say "made in Michigan," such as at Briar Rose Fibers, a stand filled with colorful yarns and even dyed wool quilt quarters.

At the Flaxcraft booth, Virginia Handy demonstrates how flax is processed. She takes interested passersby through the process from planting seeds to spinning,

Inexpensive tools are great for beginners.

Kumihimo

Kumihimo is the traditional Japanese art of cord-making, used in decorating clothing, banners, and even samurai armor. Usually done with bright colored silk, these intricate and complicated braids are both beautiful and utilitarian. Adapted for children's activities at the Michigan festival, these braids can serve as both friendship bracelets and as part of far more challenging weaving and knitting projects. Beginners often learn to braid on foam circles with markings on them, indicating the braiding pattern on the circle. As one's skills progress, there are both beautiful wooden tabletop marudai and full-sized stool ones to consider purchasing. Those who graduate to this level describe the motion of braiding to be both fluid and Zen-like. Their hands work quickly, blurring as the braid accumulates.

Tools for kumihimo aren't available at every festival, so if you're able, keep an eye out for demonstrations so you can see a skilled practitioner's hands blur and weave above the marudai. If you're interested in learning more, check out books written by Jacqui Carey or Rodrick Owen for detailed information.

Robin Russo's hands fly over a beautiful marudai available at The Spinning Studio.

weaving, or knitting the fiber. This flax demonstration stands out in a geographic area where warm animal fibers, such as sheep's wool, mohair, or alpaca are required during long winters. It's the only demonstration of its kind that I've seen at any of the festivals we've attended. However, I'm sure more than one festival attendee is wearing linen, or perhaps even spinning, knitting, or weaving it at home.

Also for the first time, I see an antique automatic rope braiding machine in motion. It churns out rope as machinery enthusiasts gather to examine several old tractors on display. Nearby, the Allegan Historical Society opens its museum grounds. The model village includes buildings and barns moved from all over the countryside to the fairgrounds. In the corner of a dusty barn filled with interesting donated artifacts, I find local hand cards, a spinning wheel or two, a hand crank sock knitter machine, and even an antique floor loom. This handmade loom, discovered in a barn, stands dusty but still draped with the rag rugs it obviously once turned out. Fiber arts are nothing new in Allegan.

At this festival, I manage to bump into friends and acquaintances from all over. They've all come to experience something that's hard to capture in words or photos. It's the breath of a welcome cool breeze in the middle of the summer, the warm enthusiasm of a crowd that feels like an extended family, and one last thing: like Brigadoon, this festival rises up, from its deeply green and fertile fruit orchards, from its small-town surroundings. It offers us all a chance to be completely immersed in the joys of sharing our skills, our fiber favorites, and our time together.

Inexpensive Tools for Spinning: A Drop Spindle

Where do clothes come from? Before there were factories, everyone spun, wove, knitted, or crocheted their clothing. For thousands of years, before the spinning wheel was invented in the Middle Ages, every yarn and thread produced for a family was spun on a spindle. Even today, people worldwide spin their yarn by hand. Many people still spin out of need. In the industrialized world, spinning offers creativity, meditation, exact control of the finished yarn, and calming, repetitive comfort.

There are gorgeous hand-turned wooden spindles for sale at festivals and online, and these are well worth the price! Yet, some people want to try spinning out before making a big expenditure. Ideal for both adults and kids, these instructions provide a basic, temporary spindle for a spontaneous spinning session. Your temporary drop spindle may not be a perfectly balanced tool, but throughout history, spinners created yarn masterpieces on many imperfect spindles. Practice makes everyone good spinners! For extensive spinning instructions and directions on making a permanent spindle, check out Connie Delaney's book, Spindle Spinning: From Novice to Expert *(Kokovoco Press, 1998).*

Skill level

Beginner

Materials

- 1 round and firm apple or potato

One of the following:

- 1 straight aluminum knitting needle, ideally between US sizes 4–9 (3.5–5.5mm); needle length can be anywhere from 8–14" (20–35.5cm)
- 1 long sharp pencil
- 1 long, strong, straight stick with a pointy end (sharpen with a pen knife or pencil sharpener)
- 1¼" (6mm) dowel, roughly 8–14" (20–35.5cm) long, sharpened at one end

- 20–30" (51–76cm) length of yarn or string to use as a leader

Fiber to spin such as:

- Medium wool roving (anyone who sells roving can help with this; it should not be too fine or slippery—avoid Merino)
- Any other fiber you have convenient, from cotton balls or batting to dog fur

Bottom whorl spindle.

Note Bear in mind that heavy spindles, such as the one you're about to make, will be best for producing thicker wool yarns. While learning, avoid using precious or expensive fiber. Save that for when you know what you're doing!

One copy each of the below free brochures, published by *Spin-Off* magazine, that cover spinning basics, or any how-to-spin book:

*   www.interweave.com/spin/resources/spinning_brochures/intro_spin.pdf

*   www.interweave.com/spin/resources/spinning_brochures/lo_tech.pdf

Instructions

Note Spinning is a physical skill, like learning to tie your shoes. It takes a little time to learn. Spin a few minutes every day on your spindle (or until the apple rots!) and within a couple of weeks, you'll be a competent spinner!

This project creates an inexpensive rudimentary, short-term, heavy spindle, ideal for teaching groups of kids or adults. If it's your goal to make lightweight yarn, you'll need a lighter weight spindle. Of course, if you want to pursue spinning seriously, it might be time in a week or two to graduate to a permanent spindle, too!

Remember to wear shoes while learning to spin. It's called a "drop spindle" for a reason, and most people drop spindles frequently while learning.

Top whorl spindle.

1. With your knitting needle or pointy stick in hand, pick up your apple or potato.

    If using the apple, look for the blossom end, opposite the stem end of the apple. With the pointy end of your needle, push the needle right through the center of the fruit. Continue pushing until the apple is 2 to 3" (5–7.6cm) away from the end of the needle.

    If using a potato, look for the center and push the needle through, as above.

2. With the point of the needle or stick facing up and the other side resting on the ground or a table, twirl your spindle. (Most spinners twist their spindle to the right, clockwise, to make yarn, and to the left, counter-clockwise, to ply.) This spindle configuration is called a "bottom whorl" spindle, because the weight is towards the bottom.

3. Holding the spindle in your hand, rotate the spindle so that the weight is at the top and the needle point is facing down. This is called a "top whorl" spindle. Choose which way feels most comfortable for you. Traditionally, bottom whorl spindles spin a little more slowly, which might be easier for a beginner, but it's really six of one, half-dozen of the other!

4. With "leader" yarn or string, make a slip knot at the end. Loop this around the pointy end of the needle or stick and shimmy it down to the top of the whorl (in this case, your apple or potato). Pull it tight, and wrap the yarn firmly around the spindle a couple of times.

5. Take time to read over the Spin-Off brochures about spinning, or, if these aren't available, look at another how-to-spin book, such as *Teach Yourself VISUALLY Handspinning* (Wiley, 2007), for how to use your leader yarn and to begin spinning.

Enjoy yourself, and remember to wash your produce after spinning and before eating!

Inexpensive Tools for Knitting: Knitting Needles

What do you need to start knitting? In the most basic sense, all you need are yarn and needles. Anyone can learn to knit, and throughout knitting history, many people have been ingenious when it comes to meeting their own knitting needs. While festivals often have every kind of knitting needle on sale, traveling to and from these events can put us in some strange and dire environments, in fact, ones without needles (gasp!) where we must knit. Here are some ways to create your own needles for yourself while traveling or for a crowd of knitting kids. Need yarn? Traditionally, one might unravel an old garment, reskein, wash, roll back into balls and—voilà—you have knitting yarn. Need needles? Sharpened wire, whittled sticks, chop sticks, pencils, or hair sticks—these have all become knitting needles in a pinch. Many folks leave a festival invigorated with new enthusiasm for fiber arts, but with limited resources. If you're not handy, consider checking out yard sales and thrift shops for yarn and needles others have given away. If you like the idea of making your own, here are some approaches to making low tech tools that won't break the bank.

Skill level

Beginner

Materials

- Two sticks of equal girth such as:
  Chopsticks
  Hair sticks
  Even lengths of dowel
  Lengths of stiff wire
  Pencils
- If sticks need to have points created: a pencil sharpener or pen knife
- If sticks have any rough edges: fine sandpaper or a nail file or a city sidewalk
- If sticks need to be cut to the right length: a coping saw or other handsaw
- A needle size gauge
- Two beads, erasers, clay, or other substance to create needle ends (optional)
- Craft or wood glue

Gauge

Your needles and yarn weight will control the gauge of your future knitting. Keep this in mind if you have a specific project in mind for your needles.

Instructions

1. Your raw materials for needles will determine much about what you'll need to do to transform them into knitting needles. With hair sticks, go directly to #6. With pencils, chopsticks, or wire, go directly to #4. For dowels, proceed as follows:

2. Bring your needle gauge to the hardware store while purchasing dowels. Buy one long dowel for each set of needles desired, using the needle gauge to determine the size of new needles.

3. Use saw to trim dowels to desired lengths. Knitting needles traditionally come in lengths of 6, 8, 10, 12, or 14" (15.3, 20.3, 25.4, 30.5, 35.5cm), but length is entirely up to you.

4. Using a pencil sharpener or pen knife, carefully sharpen the edges of your needles if necessary. Try to create two points that match. This is also the chance to create blunt tips for splitty yarns, or very pointy tips for lace knitting. This is your preference.

5. Using sandpaper, a nail file, or even a sidewalk, carefully sand down any areas of your needles that are not smooth. To test for smoothness, take a bit of yarn and run it over the needle. If the yarn catches, the needle isn't smooth enough. Most needles will also become smoother with time due to oils from one's hands as knitting takes place.

6. Not all needles have a stopper or cap on the end of the needle. However, if you'd like one, use a bead, eraser, or clay to go on the end of the needle. Secure this with glue.

Finishing

Use the needle gauge to figure out approximately what size your new needles are, for the sake of convenience. Make a note of the size. Some people even choose to write this on their needles. If your needles are somewhere in between traditional sizes, this is not a problem. In fact, the knitting needle industry is not widely standardized. Even with commercially made needles, it is easiest to know approximately what size the needles are, by doing a gauge swatch, and use this to determine if the needles will work for the yarn and pattern.

Creating a Skein

Skeins or hanks are great ways to store yarn. Yarn wound into balls can sometimes stretch or deteriorate because it is under tension. Many spinners and some knitters rely on skeins for storage, washing, and dyeing yarns. A niddy-noddy and a swift are both standard devices for making and working with skeins, but even the backs of two chairs will suffice if you need to make a large skein and you happen to have no specialized equipment nearby.

What if you have none of that equipment and you're camping at a festival? Spinning at a guild event outside? Well, you could get up and ask around for help—spinners and knitters are friendly and might loan you what you need, but there's an even more basic way to make a skein. The following is useful for everyone, but especially handy for those who use drop spindles.

Hold up one of your arms so your elbow is bent and your fingers and thumb point to the sky, making a right angle or V-shape. Tuck one end of yarn and hold down with your thumb. With your other hand, loosely wrap the yarn down your arm and around your bent elbow. Bring the yarn loosely back up the other side, looping the yarn between your thumb and fingers, in that V-shape. Continue on in the same direction until you're finished making the skein. Tie the end of the yarn to the end you've tucked down with your thumb. Make sure to tie off the skein in one or two other places. Use your other hand to take the skein off your arm.

Be careful to skein loosely, or you may be trapped! How many yards or meters is your newly wound skein? Use a tape measure and wrap it around your arm in the same way to make one skein length. Count the number of strands of yarn in the skein and multiply it by your measurement to find the number of yards or meters in your new skein.

chapter 7

Heart of America Sheep Show and Fiber Fest

Sedalia, Missouri is the home of a famous Scott Joplin ragtime festival. It's also the new home of the Heart of America Sheep Show and Fiber Fest. This festival has been held in a variety of places in Missouri. It is now held at the Missouri State Fairgrounds. This is the largest fairgrounds in the USA, on 396 acres of buildings, campgrounds, and exhibits. The spacious facilities allow for easy parking, camping, and room for animals and children to romp. The entire indoor event takes place in the historic Swine Pavilion, one of the many buildings on the campus. This building offers shelter from spring thunderstorms and the best open air ventilation imaginable for a festival. (Pigs don't do well in the heat.) On further reflection, it should be called the Swine Palace. It's just that grand!

Along one long open aisle, the class areas are lined up, one after another. Classes for both adults and children run nearly continuously, alongside demonstrations, vendor booths, and fleece, rabbit, and other competitions for three days. The open arrangement of the classes allows bystanders to check out twined rug weaving, needle felting, knitting, spinning, bobbin lace and other activities. Family members drop by to see their relatives taking classes in the relaxed atmosphere of the fair. Unlike the strict "no dog" prohibition of some festivals, well-behaved dogs on leads wander and rest alongside spinning wheels at their owners' sides.

The emphasis at this festival is on learning. While there are animal events (including breed competitions, a fleece judging, and silent auction), the competition is downplayed. Even with animals brought to be sold from near and far—sharing, learning, and visiting remain the emphasis of this festival. The event, put on by the Missouri Natural Colored Wool Growers Association (MONCWGA), is very well organized. Each class starts and ends on time, the booths are neatly labeled, and the animals on display are brought in with a minimum of fuss and a lot of loving care. As one of the organizers

Alex Wilcoxon concentrates on learning in her bobbin lace class.

pointed out, in other years, the sheep aspect of the festival was more prominent, but as gas prices go up, shepherds feel less motivated to travel long distances with their sheep. In order to keep up the interest in the festival with fewer animal competitions, the focus has switched to holding lots of classes. Why hold lots of classes? Everyone enjoys learning something new.

Many festivals have classes, and in this regard, Heart of America is not special. What is outstanding is that every class is financially affordable, and every level of student, from beginner to expert, feels welcome. Missouri is lucky to have active fiber arts guilds and gatherings throughout the state. MONCWGA mines these guilds to find good teachers in every field.

The atmosphere is so relaxed and open to learning that when I decide at 12:58 pm, to take a class at 1 pm, I pay my $30 fee without penalty or rebuke. Zelma Cleaveland, the instructor, sees me coming her way dragging a spinning wheel, and I'm welcomed with a smile. I'm all set to take a nearly 3-hour spinning class on "Llama: A Fiber for All Seasons." Every class member learns something new, all are praised for their contributions, and I leave with a good feeling of knowing more than just new information. I know new friends.

The New U.S. Lamb Market

Fifteen years ago, Tom Parry and his wife went to Kansas City to do a shearing demonstration. Carolyn Parry was doing the shearing while her husband was approached by a taxi driver. He asked if he might come out to their farm to buy and slaughter his own lamb. Farmers sell lambs every year both in order to keep afloat financially and to keep their flock size manageable. However, farmers are often at the mercy of poor local livestock prices, so Mr. Parry was happy to consider selling lambs this way. Soon, the taxi driver visited the farm with his wife and three small children, who were 6 months, 2 years and 4 years of age at the time. The taxi driver was Muslim and wanted to perform the *Eid al-Adha* (ritual of sacrifice), in which one slaughters an animal (camel, cow, sheep, or goat) and gives away much of the meat to charity and to community members.

The experience was meaningful to that taxi driver, and he told his friends. Mr. Parry developed a business in which he would sell lambs, to be slaughtered on the farm, to Muslims seeking to fulfill their holiday religious obligations. As in any religious community, word of Mr. Parry's good lambs and kind manner spread, and now he has customers who travel from as far away as Detroit to visit his Missouri farm. Every year, an imam and a van load of Muslim women come from Detroit to ritually slaughter several lambs. When the imams visit the farm, they go to each corner of it to bless it—which of course Mr. Parry is happy to accommodate, since he feels his farm needs all the blessing it can get!

These days, much of the Parry's best business at Vinegar Hill Farm comes from this very different kind of lamb market. The taxi driver still visits, but his 4-year-old child is now in college!

Carolyn Parry demonstrates a way to blade shear on a sheep stand.

Every Missourian I meet at Heart of America is enthusiastic and excited to tell me about the fiber arts riches of the state. More than a few don't hesitate to tell me about their wineries, cattle farming issues, and local events, as well as about fiber arts. I'm instantly a part of this warm statewide community, including being welcomed by the master of ceremonies at the Saturday night "Hoo Rah" and invited to come back soon. Sorely tempted by local vendors' wares such as Hillcreek Fiber Studio's looms, Tongue River Farm's Icelandic yarns and fibers, and more distant delights such as Louisiana's Running Moon Farm's spindles, I'm barely able to restrain my spending.

Anna Wright and her angora goat in the show ring.

Even without buying everything I'd like, I come home richer, simply by talking more, learning more, and taking in the sight of so many fiber animals—Angora rabbits, llamas, Shetland sheep and tame Pygora goats all compete for most fuzzy, cute, and furry. Meanwhile, every shepherd shows me a new reason to appreciate their beloved animals. A fashion show allows everyone to vote and celebrate participants' newest creations: felting, knitting, spinning, crochet, sewing, and Indian beadwork. The animals are fêted as well, with lots of ribbons for adults and children who show their animals off with pride.

On Saturday night, the shouts of celebration at the huge potluck supper, the Phelps Family Band's bluegrass and the baas of sheep echo in my ears, keeping me company with warm thoughts about Missouri, the Show Me State, and its rich fiber arts community on the long drive home.

Running Moon Farm's spindles.

Sit Upon: A Crocheted Wool Roving Seat Pad

If you were in Girl Scouts as a child, you might have sat on a little cushion or mat at meetings called a "Sit Upon." This is the festival version—ideal for metal folding chairs, the fairgrounds' hard concrete floors or benches, or sitting on the bleachers to watch competitions. At home, it can be dressed up into seat pads for your dining room, a yoga meditation cushion, or even a placemat for your dog's water bowl. Don't hesitate to get creative with this one! A larger mat can be felted for a firmer texture, or crochet it much bigger, add some rubber backing and you'll have a fabulous rug or dog bed.

Skill level

Easy

Finished Measurements

Circular pad: 15" (38cm) diameter

Square pad: 14" (35.5 cm) square

Adjust size to fit your chair and bottom needs!

Materials

- 5–6 oz. (140–170g) of medium to coarse wool roving makes 1 Circular or Square Sit Upon
- 3–4 oz. (85–113g) each of 2 colors of medium to coarse wool roving makes 1 two-color Circular Sit Upon

Suggested wool breeds include: coarse Romney, Icelandic, Karakul, Cotswold, or Shetland

Note Talk to any festival vendor with roving for sale and you'll be steered in the right direction if you ask for medium to coarse wools.

Samples made with: naturally gray Romney roving, cranberry and teal-dyed Cotswold roving, and green-dyed medium-coarse mixed breed roving

- US size Q (16mm) crochet hook or size to create a firm fabric
- 1 stitch marker
- Extra large tapestry needle or smaller crochet hook to weave in ends

Gauge

4 sc and 4 rows = 4" (10cm) for Circular Sit Upon

3 sc and 2 rows = 4" (10cm) for Square Sit Upon

Gauge is approximate here—roving density varies greatly. Use your best judgment and work to create a firm fabric.

Instructions

Note *Working with unspun roving is an art and not a science. As long as your Sit Upon is roughly flat and firm, you're doing fine! If roving comes apart, simply join a new piece by picking it up with crochet hook and working in the ends as described in the Finishing section. Wool is naturally "sticky" and should hold together. As an alternative to roving, you can use scrap yarns to create much the same effect, but plan on using multiple strands of yarn to create a suitably bulky texture.*

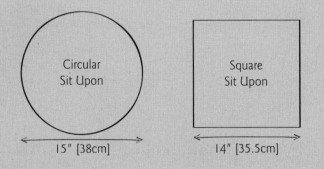

Circular Sit Upon — 15" [38cm]

Square Sit Upon — 14" [35.5cm]

Circular Sit Upon

Sit Upon is worked in a continuous spiral. Do not join rounds *except as specified*. Use a marker to keep track of the beg of the rnd.

Note *To create a spiral 2-color Sit Upon, alternate colors with each rnd.*

With crochet hook and roving, make a slip knot and ch 5. Join with a sl st into the first ch to form a ring (sl st counts as 1 st). Make 2 more ch sts—8 sts total. Place marker for beg of the rnd.

Rnd 1: Work 2 sc into each st—16 sts.

Rnd 2: *Sc in next st, 2 sc in next st; rep from * to end of rnd—24 sts.

Rnd 3: *Sc in next 2 sts, 2 sc in next st; rep from * to end of rnd—32 sts.

Rnd 4: *Sc in next 3 sts, 2 sc in next st; rep from * to end of rnd—40 sts.

Continue on this way, steadily increasing the number of sts between increases, until the Sit Upon's diameter measures 15" (38cm) or desired size. Sl st to join. Fasten off and weave in ends, taking care to make the circular join as smooth as possible.

Square Sit Upon

With crochet hook and roving, make a slip knot and ch 12.

*Ch1; turn work.

Skipping first st, dc in each st across—11 dc.

Rep from *.

When work appears square or roughly 14" (35.5cm), fasten off at end of row.

Finishing

Weave in roving ends with your fingers, a crochet hook, or a very large-eyed tapestry needle. If the roving seems to create a bump, separate the ends into 2 smaller strands and weave them in separately.

Icelandic Winter Cap

This unisex cap knits up quickly and creates a halo of warmth. The ribbing can stretch to fit a variety of hair-styles, and the brim is just snug enough to cling to your ears in a big breeze. This naturally colored sample, knit in Icelandic wool from Tongue River Farm in Missouri, has a special glow and earthy appeal. Sadly, Susan Briggs, the farm's owner, passed away as this book went to press. Her natural-color Icelandic yarn is now available from Bloomin' Acres farm. Substitute Reynolds Lopi if you'd like a whole rainbow of dyed colors.

Skill level

Intermediate

Size

S (L)

Finished Measurements

To fit head sizes: 20½ (23)" (51.25 [57.5]cm)

Materials

- 150 yd. (137m) of any bulky weight yarn that knits at with the appropriate gauge

Sample knit with: Tongue River Farm *Icelandic Lopi Yarn* (100 percent Icelandic wool; 150 yd. [137m] per 5 oz. [140g] skein): color Medium Blue Gray, 1 skein

- US size 10 (6mm) double-pointed needles *or size to obtain gauge*

- US size 10 (6mm) circular needle, 16" (41cm) long (optional)

- 1 stitch marker

- Tapestry needle

Gauge

14 sts and 18 rows = 4" (10cm) in St st

Pattern Stitches

Ribbing
Worked over a multiple of 4 sts.

All rnds: *K2, p2; rep from * to end of rnd.

Instructions

Note This hat is knit from the crown downward and may be adjusted in length by working additional rounds before the band.

Using 1 dpn, cast on 4 sts.

Setup row: Inc 1 in each st—8 sts.

Distribute sts on 3 or 4 dpns (entirely your preference), join to work in the round being careful not to twist sts, and place marker to indicate beg of rnd.

Setup rnd: Inc 1 in each st—16 sts.

Rnd 1: *K1, inc 1, rep from * to end of rnd—24 sts.

Rnd 2: *K2, inc 1, rep from * to end of rnd—32 sts.

Rnd 3: *K3, Inc 1, rep from * to end of rnd—40 sts.

Cont in this way, inc 8 sts evenly in each rnd, until there are 72 (80) sts, changing to circular needle if desired.

Work K2, P2 Ribbing for 6" (15cm), until length from crown to edge of work measures 8" (20.5cm), or until hat is desired length.

Band

Work 4 rnds in the following sl st patt to make the hat band:

Rnds 1–4: *Slip 2 sts knitwise, p2; rep from * to end of rnd.

Rnds 5–8: Knit.

Rnd 9: Purl.

Bind off. Brim will roll up.

Finishing

Weave in ends. If desired, sew rolled brim in place for a firmer edging.

This hat can also be slightly fulled in order to make it more windproof by gently handwashing and agitating the hat in hot soapy water. Take care not to shrink it too much in this process!

chapter 8
Shearing Day

At nearly every fiber festival, there's a sheep shearing demonstration. A farmer saves a few sheep to be shorn "for show," so onlookers understand how shearing works. Yet, every year, all over the world, nearly every wool-producing sheep is shorn on its own farm. Most sheep shearings happen on private farms, with little fuss or fanfare. This makes it even more special to be invited to a local farm's sheep shearing.

Although city slickers may assume "there's a machine to do this," that just isn't the case. As Stephanie Pearl-McPhee, aka the Yarn Harlot, points out, every sheep, is shorn by hand. This is done either with old fashioned sharp sheep shears, or much more commonly, with an electric shear. This looks like an electric razor for sheep. It comes complete with different sharp toothed combs for shearing the wide variety of sheep breeds and other fiber animals.

Shearers on New Zealand's and Australia's sheep stations (where an average sheep station can contain thousands of sheep) are known for their incredibly fast work, shearing enormous numbers of sheep at an unbelievable average rate of 45 seconds a sheep. In March of 2007, Rod Sutton of New Zealand sheared more than 720 sheep in a day, but in the United States, the average number of sheep on a farm is usually much smaller. Most shearers in the United States work more slowly, but are often responsible for catching the sheep before shearing, and administering medicine and trimming their hooves afterwards.

I've attended or helped out at sheep shearings in Kentucky, New York, and North Carolina. In every instance, the invitation is timed to coincide with when a shearer can visit the farm, and not at the farmer's convenience. Shearers in the USA are in demand and travel long distances to hundreds of farms a year. Most sheep are shorn in spring before lambing, or alternately, in the fall, and these are busy times of year for a shearer.

Everyone hopes for dry weather. Even if the shearing will take place indoors, it's a bad idea to attempt sheep shearing in the rain. The wool will absorb moisture, making it prone to mildew and mold. The shearer and other helpers risk slipping while wrestling damp sheep in potentially muddy or wet barns and fields. Sometimes the shearing is postponed at the last minute, called off just like a ball game for weather.

In Kentucky, I'm lucky to have a friend who invites me to his farm every year in May for shearing day. Bestefar Farm, owned by Albert Petersen, a retired Geography professor, is just a few miles away from my house. Albert keeps Romney and Romney cross sheep and has a flock of about 20. Every year, Gerald Crowe, a shearer, comes to shear. Gerald travels widely across Kentucky, Tennessee and Virginia, shearing lots of sheep, as well as llamas, alpacas, and angora goats. Shearing is very hard on the body, requiring a lot of bending and lifting. A good

Handspinner Mina Doerner and her daughter Linnaea skirt a fleece.

Gerald Crowe shears a ewe.

rams struggle and fight the shearer. Sometimes it takes two people to position them into place.

Gerald estimates what the animal weighs, and Albert prepares the wormer medicine, used in warmer parts of the country to keep the sheep free from parasites. When the medicine is administered, Gerald trims the ewe's toe nails, and she hops to her feet, racing to the pasture. Out in the field, the sheep don't recognize each other without their fleeces. They baa loudly, calling out to identify one another.

At most farms, shearing day is an entirely outdoor event. If you go indoors to use the bathroom, remember to take off your dirty shoes to help keep the shepherd's home clean! If there are curious children present, parents have to be alert to keep them out of the way. Every adult must be prepared to lend a hand if necessary. A skittish young ewe or an aggressive ram can be dangerous…and nearly all Angora goats can be wily!

Some farms raise their sheep with fiber in mind, and skirt fleeces on shearing day, removing undesirable bits of manure and coarse wool and preparing it for hand-spinners. Other farmers raise them for meat, keeping their sheep as pets or as live lawn mowers. The wool is not always useful to them. At Bestefar Farm, Gerald rolls up most of the wool and stuffs it into an enormous sack, keeping an eye out for nice fleeces for me as a present.

shearer also has a steady hand and a calming way with animals, and must be flexible to cope with a wide variety of conditions on the farms he or she visits.

Often friends drop by to watch and visit while the sheep are shorn. Albert's helper Courtney helps to usher each sheep out of the holding pen and onto the shearing floor. Gerald is relaxed and competent, offering to teach others to shear and talking about each animal as he gives her the annual haircut. Each sheep is maneuvered onto its tail, where it sits, gently manipulated by Gerald's legs, arms and body movements during shearing. Older sheep deal with this calmly, anticipating the cool feeling they'll have when it's over. Like kids facing a first haircut, younger ewes that haven't been sheared before and feisty

Lambs and ewes in the pasture.

Otherwise, the wool leaves in his truck when he's finished shearing. Some years, Gerald takes the wool and some lambs as part or all of his payment. Gerald sells some hand spinning fleeces himself, and brings the rest to the regional wool pool.

Hand spinning and yarn production use only a small amount of American wool production. Most U. S. wool production is sold in an industrial wool pool. That wool must be white, and is sorted and classified according to its coarseness and quality. The farmer is paid by the pound, and while the amount varies based on the global wool market, it's usually far less than a dollar a pound. Since the wool pool doesn't take "black wool," colored wool of all kinds is often widely available to spinners.

Sometimes the cost of paying the shearer can exceed the profit from the wool pool. Even when a farmer has a breed of sheep intended only for meat, those sheep must be shorn for their health; they will overheat and die if they aren't shorn regularly. Luckily, every kind of wool has a purpose, from men's suits to industrial felt car trunk liners.

Joanne Seiff spins outside in the sunshine.

Albert Petersen and Linnaea Doerner visit with the bottle-fed lambs.

When shearing is over for the year, the farmer settles up with the shearer, and they share a cold drink or a meal. Everyone lingers, watching the scene as the neatly shorn sheep return to grazing their pasture and mothers find their lambs. Every so often, a ewe might give birth but then won't be able to feed her lamb, and Albert will raise the lamb himself with a bottle. When this happens, he'll take time after the shearing is over to let us visit with the lamb. He'll help the youngest child visiting to offer the lamb a bottle on her own.

I love spinning a freshly shorn fleece and will rush home to skirt, wash, and process the wool. Sometimes I leave a bit unwashed. Sitting in the spring sunshine in my yard, I'll spin directly from the lock, without carding or combing the wool, feeling the warm sheepy fibers glide into yarn on my spinning wheel. If there's too much wool for me to process at home, I'll stay in my dirty shearing clothes until everything is skirted and ready for me to send off to my favorite fiber mill. Every year, I bring a gift, perhaps a handspun handknit hat, some jam, or a book on sheep to Albert to thank him for the fleeces he gives me, and for inviting me to visit Bestefar Farm. I love shearing day!

Preparing for and Helping at a Sheep Shearing

Even if you never attend a shearing, it's nice to know where your wool comes from. Every single fleece in the world is shorn by a shearer. These sheep "barbers" travel hundreds of miles to farms and festivals all over the country to keep sheep cool and healthy by helping to harvest fleeces. For the handspinner, there is nothing more exciting than a beautiful, freshly shorn fleece. Spinning with a "fresh" fleece is like buying fresh bread from a neighborhood bakery. You identify with the baker (the shepherd), the ingredients (the farm and sheep) and the taste of the bread or the enjoyment of your fleece is richer for the connection. Choosing your fleece while it's still "on the hoof" and participating in shearing day are special treats. For the new shepherd, it's helpful to know exactly how this big day on the farm will work. This is a rough how-to for those of us who've been invited to attend but don't quite know what to expect.

Materials

- Sheep
- Covered sheep pen
- Open space for shearer, preferably with electricity nearby
- Shearing board (optional)
- Sheets or bags for fleece
- Skirting table (optional)
- Sheep hoof trimmer (optional)
- Wormer (optional)

Instructions

Note Wear work clothes, including long pants and sturdy, closed-toe shoes to a shearing. You may need to help!

1. **Prepare the sheep:** Sheep are usually shorn once in the spring or twice a year, spring and fall, depending on the breed and the weather conditions of your local area. Round up the sheep and keep them in a covered sheep pen the night before shearing day. This helps dry out fleeces in case of rain. Also, keep the sheep off their feed or grass for a little while. As one

might imagine, shearing day can be stressful. It's helpful for sheep to have a mostly empty stomach to keep them from soiling their own fleeces as they are being shorn.

2. **Prepare the area:** The shearer will likely bring his or her own shearing board. This is often a large piece of plywood that creates an official shearing space. Most shearers use electric shears. These shears have a very long cord and need to be plugged in. Often the shearers hook the shearing cord over a rafter so that the cord hangs from above. This keeps both the shearer and nervous sheep safe from any kind of equipment accident.

3. **Bring the sheep, one at a time, to be shorn:** The most exciting part of shearing is usually wrestling the anxious sheep, one at
a time, from the holding pen to the shearing board. To keep the shearer working steadily, other helpers are usually appointed to help with this job. If a sheep has horns, it's OK to lead the sheep gently by the horns.

4. **Watch for safety:** Shearing sheep requires concentration, strength, and skill. Usually a shearer can handle even a large ewe or wether on his or her own. (A wether is a castrated male sheep, usually kept exclusively for wool production.) Once the sheep is positioned correctly (on its hind quarters) it is somewhat immobilized and patient while it's being shorn. Sometimes a shearer will need help with a large ram. For safety's sake, never let a child or an inexperienced animal handler help with a ram. Rams can be dangerous.

5. **Shear the sheep:** Shearing a sheep can take anywhere from 3 to 20 minutes, depending on the shearer's experience, the animal's size and nature, and whether the shearer is using traditional handshears or an electric shear. During this time, it's not a good idea to dart onto the shearing board for any reason . . . not even to evaluate a fleece or sweep the board. A shearer will let you know if you are needed to help.

Tom Barr demonstrates shearing at the Taos Wool Festival.

Gerald Crowe shows Joanne Seiff how it's done.

6. **Collect the fleece:** Immediately after the animal is shorn, the fleece can be whisked away for skirting, if there are enough people available to help with this. (See instructions for Skirting a Fleece, p. 98, for more details.) If not, the fleece may be moved away from the shearer as she and the shepherd attend to the sheep's needs.

7. **Check the sheep:** Most sheep growers use shearing day as an opportunity to evaluate their flock. The sheep is examined quickly for any potential health problems. The animal's hooves are trimmed to keep its feet healthy. Often, the sheep is then dosed with wormer to keep it safe from parasites.

8. **Guide the sheep back to the pasture:** As soon as the shearer and shepherd are finished with the sheep, it struggles to its feet and rushes out to its pasture. Sometimes it needs a little guidance in finding the gate. Observers can guide a sheep back to its pasture simply by fanning out behind it and helping it find its way out.

9. **Skirt the fleece:** If skirting isn't taking place during shearing day, a professional shearer can do rough skirting and roll up a fleece in just a few moments. Fleeces vary enormously in size, weighing anywhere from 2 to 15 pounds, depending on the breed of sheep, size of animal, and when it was last shorn.

Finishing

Depending on the number of shearers and helpers and the size of the flock, shearing can take a long time. Even if you're not helping with animal care or shearing itself, everyone appreciates an extra hand to sweep away debris, provide water or food, or help with the skirting and storage of the fleeces. If you're invited to someone's farm to help, try to stay as long as you're needed.

At the end of the day, the sheep pen will need to be cleaned, the shearer fed and paid, and places found for all the fleeces. If you're lucky enough to go home with a fleece, you'll have the pleasure of working with a fiber that's as fresh as possible!

Skirting a Fleece

When faced with a raw fleece, spinners and felters will want to sort the wool before sending the fiber away for processing or washing it at home. The undesirable bits of manure and coarse edges of a fleece are removed as well, and the term "skirting" refers to this process of sorting and removing wool that isn't right for spinning. Sheep and freshly shorn wool have an aroma all their own, a mixture of barnyard, sweet hay, and an earthy, live animal scent. It's a rich odor that lingers—so it's best to skirt fleeces outside if possible.

If you've never skirted a fleece before, it's useful to have some basic suggestions for your first time. Shearers, farmers, and spinners all have different specifications for their wool, so skirting can take 5 to 45 minutes, depending on the fleece and its intended use. Whether you're skirting with others on shearing day or by yourself, this will help you get started!

Materials

- Old clothes
- Well-ventilated flat area (preferably outdoors)
- Large, waist-high skirting table (optional)
- Old bed sheet
- 1 raw fleece
- Pillow case or other cloth bag for fleece
- Trash bag

Instructions

Note Every spinner, farmer, and shearer will have different skirting preferences. If you are skirting fleeces for someone else, be sure to ask questions as to what they think is worth keeping or should be culled.

1. While wearing old clothes, spread out an old bed sheet on a large skirting table or on the ground. (Be sure the ground is as free from leaves, grass clippings, and other detritus as possible.)

2. Spread out only one fleece at a time. Fleeces are wrapped in a specific way by a good shearer. It often looks like a sleeping bag, with the cut ends on the outside. When the fleece is unrolled, it should look like a large shag rug, with the weathered tips on view and the cut ends underneath. Some sheep breeds will have fleeces that maintain their shape, and will look like a pelt. Others will not hold together as well. Do the best you can to lay out the fleece neatly at this stage.

3. Remove any manure-tags, stained wool, or unusable wool from the edges of the fleece. This is often belly wool, and it's been in some unsavory places. Much of this can go directly into your trash bag to be thrown away. If you are a gardener, you can soak this wool and create your own "compost tea" for your plants. You can even put this waste wool on your garden as mulch, but beware—if you have any domestic animals around (dogs, cats, goats, etc.) they could ingest this, and it could make them ill.

4. Look for "britch" wool. This is from the tail area of the sheep, and is often very coarse, dirty or "kempy." What this means is that you'll sometimes see hairiness to this fiber. It can be saved for use in something that will see hard wear (rugs, warp yarn, etc.) or again, thrown away if it is not useful for your purposes.

5. Remove any obvious vegetable matter. For instance, burrs are impossible to process with carding machinery of any kind—best to throw these parts out right away. Sometimes you can shake a fleece and remove bits of hay and seed. Shaking the fleece will also help remove any second cuts. Second cuts are small short bits of fiber caused by a shearer who doesn't shear the fleece acceptably on the first try; they will result in pills and neps in your spinning or carding if not removed.

6. Sort the fleece. The best wool on any fleece will be the shoulder wool (see illustration); however, most modern sheep breeding works to create uniformity across a fleece. If your fleece looks relatively uniform and you plan to have it processed professionally or will adequately intermix the fibers on your own, it's probably unnecessary to sort further for most practical uses.

Joanne Seiff and Mina Doerner shake a fleece.

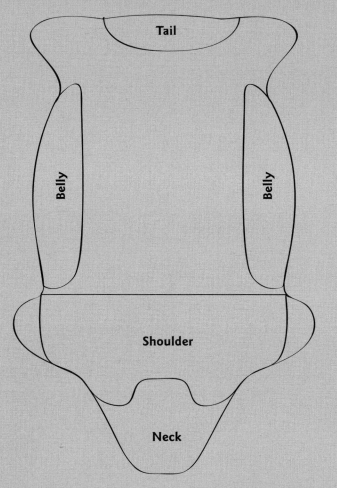

Historically, different parts of the fleece were subdivided even further for use in different projects. Primitive breeds of sheep such as Icelandic, Shetland, or Karakul may well have very different sorts of wool on different parts of their bodies. In this case, it might be worthwhile to examine the fleece and subdivide it into categories based on the character of the fleece, such as crimp, length of the staple, and coarseness. Each sorted category should then be kept separately and processed for projects that best suit the wool's character. While traditional sources warn that mixing vastly different fibers can cause irregular shrinkage or uneven dyeing; most of today's handspinners encounter this only with a fleece that truly lacks uniformity.

For further information on historic wool sorting, consult Elsie Davenport's book, *Your Handspinning* (Select Books, 1964).

Finishing

When a fleece is adequately skirted to meet your needs, store it in a pillow case or any kind of natural fiber cloth breathable bag. (You can find an ample supply of old sheets for this sort of thing at a local thrift store.) Avoid plastic for any kind of long term storage, because as temperature and humidity changes, the fleece, filled with lanolin and *suint* (sheep sweat) will become damp and possibly mold or rot.

Many spinners proceed directly at this point to wash the fleece, or to send it away to a woolen mill for washing, picking, and carding. If you plan to store raw fleece for any length of time, bear in mind that wool moths are most attracted to strong smelling fiber. To deter moths, store your raw fleece in a bright sunny location. Air and rotate the fleece frequently. If desired, cloak the odor with cedar, lavender, or pennyroyal to mask the smell that, to moths, is an incredibly appealing scent.

Warning Do not use pennyroyal or lavender if you are pregnant or thinking of becoming pregnant. Both can cause miscarriage.

West

chapter 9
Black Sheep Gathering

If you love colored sheep and fleece, and party hard, Black Sheep Gathering in Eugene, Oregon is the festival for you. Once upon a time in U. S. breeding circles, no shepherd worth his or her salt wanted a sheep with a "black" fleece. Black fleece, also called colored fleece, means any color that isn't white. Just like the jokes about the family's black sheep, a shepherd risked "contaminating" his flock's genes if colored sheep bred with white ones. White wool brought in the best money; gray, tan, cinnamon, black, and chocolate brown wool all ended up being thrown out.

In contrast, handspinners, have always valued colored fleeces for their rich colors and ease of use. No dyeing necessary for these fleeces; they come already colored! Or, if you want to produce a rich jewel tone, nothing is better to start with than a gray fleece. Who started this trend? There are many people who always valued a colored fleece, but Morris Culver was the first to import two colored Romney rams from Britain to create his Oregon flock. He was ostracized. At shows and events, his sheep were quarantined in a separate part of the show barn, so his colored animals wouldn't "contaminate" the pristine white flocks. When Morris told this tale, he'd laugh and we'd all share a good joke about the birds and the bees. We wondered if those shepherds, 50 some years ago, missed a crucial biology lesson.

How things change! Morris Culver lived to see his beloved colors become popular, and traveled the country judging fleece and animal competitions. In Oregon, on

One of many "black sheep" at Black Sheep Gathering.

Morris' home turf, a three-day event of large proportion celebrates what used to be the odd child out, the black sheep. Morris Culver's tradition continues; new breeding programs from Britain offer American spinners access to Teeswater, Wensleydale, Gotland, and other popular but rare sheep breeds. Meanwhile, Black Sheep, as this gathering is affectionately called, plays host to some of the most talented fiber artists, woodworkers, and other fiber-oriented vendors in the West.

Want an olive wood, ebony, or even a glass spindle? A one of a kind antique or new wheel? Black Sheep is the place. Of course, there are vendors that carry the same knitting needles, yarns, and other necessities across the country, but in Oregon, I saw many tools, yarns, and fibers for the first time. Whether it was a Betty Roberts spinning wheel, made from exotic woods with wild flowers and butterflies laminated in, or an antique sock knitter, this gathering was full of special, handmade, and cherished items.

This festival isn't just about equipment. The public wool show, judged by Judith MacKenzie McCuin when I attended, was an outstanding event. Much like attending a symphony, people sat in chairs arranged in semi-circles in front of the judge as she talked about fleece. All day on Friday and part of the day Saturday, anyone could attend. The quiet was like the hush between movements at a classical music performance. People sat in chairs, spinning or taking notes, learning at the feet of an expert.

Even the nearby wool show sale is intoxicating. Nearly every fleece is spotless and a spinner's dream. Any serious spinner could get drunk on the fumes! The crowd oohs and ahhs over the incredible array of color and fleece, texture

Wool roving for spinning in every color.

The very popular Socks That Rock yarn is available from the Blue Moon Fiber Arts stall.

every tailgate party. In motels near the fairgrounds, the open-door-party feel continues, with fibery folks bouncing from room to room, sharing pie, fabulous finds, and spinning and knitting to all hours of the night. These spinners and knitters party hard!

On Saturday night, several hundred people gather to celebrate the 30th anniversary of the Natural Colored Wool Growers Association. With wine glasses or spindles in hand, many toast the legacy of Morris Culver, and the great successes of colored sheep in the United States. A Spinner's Lead fashion show takes place, in which intricate wool creations, handspun or felted, knitted or crocheted, take center stage, as handspinners show off their creations, with a sheep, often decorated as well, in tow.

This gathering doesn't just celebrate black sheep. It celebrates the people who love black sheep, those who worship at the church of wool. At most festivals, the only people to stay all day are the vendors and the shepherds. At Black Sheep, most of the attendees finish shopping or taking classes, but they don't go home. Instead, they draw up a chair, and join in making community, knitting, and spinning, making and meeting friends. All are welcome here…it's a loving, large, open party that celebrates the people in Oregon and the artistry that made this strong Pacific Northwest fiber community possible.

and style. Even the fleece sale volunteer spins a textured mohair yarn on a silk binder that makes me want to touch and fondle it.

When the judging is over, people line up across the parking lot to grab their special treasure, a perfect fleece. Competition is fierce as the crowd rushes inside. Although there are many exquisite white fleeces, it's the black sheep fleeces that reign supreme.

The party continues in the parking lot, where impromptu groups of spinners sit near RV's, chatting a mile a minute, sharing glasses of wine and conversation. It feels just like a rock concert with groupies gushing at

Judith MacKenzie McCuin teaches while judging fleece at the wool show.

The Woolen Mill

Thomas Kay Woolen Mill in Salem, Oregon.

An essential part of the U. S. fiber arts tradition is the woolen mill. Many people know the history of the New England textile mills, but few realize that in many new settlements, woolen mills were a necessity for the pioneers. As the frontier moved westward, there's evidence that pioneers built industrial-sized woolen mills in many communities. For instance, in the late eighteenth century, Bowling Green, Kentucky's first woolen mill was situated inside Lost River Cave, powered by the water of an underground river.

Oregon was no different. White settlers discovered early on that the Pacific Northwest was an ideal place to raise sheep. As a result, Thomas Kay started his woolen mill in 1889 in Salem, Oregon. This mill, powered by a canal dug from the nearby river, created work for the community and processed the enormous quantity of local fleeces sheared each year. From washing and dyeing to picking, carding, spinning, and weaving, it was all done in one large building in downtown Salem.

This mill clothed the lumberjacks and the Alaskan gold miners, as well as provided army blankets and other wartime essentials during both world wars. Sadly, the rise in synthetics and imports closed the mill down for good in 1962, but some of Thomas Kay's descendants are still in the wool mill business at Pendleton Mills. These days, you can visit Thomas Kay's mill at the Mission Mill Museum, an hour away from Black Sheep Gathering, to see the rich history of Oregon's wool tradition.

At Black Sheep Gathering and at many other festivals, the industrial wool mill's descendants are present. These modern-day mills are often smaller affairs, but the handspinner or shepherd uses them frequently to have his or her wool "processed." Buy a raw fleece (or five) and don't have time to wash it? These mills allow busy fiber artists to pick their processing needs. All over the country, you can find someone to wash, pick, card, or comb, and even spin, felt, or weave your fiber into the materials you want to use.

Washed wool is on display, ready for the carding machines.

Fishtail Vest

If there is a single symbol of the natural vitality of the Pacific Northwest, it is probably the salmon. The life-long journey of the salmon begins high in the mountain streams, where dying parents lay and fertilize eggs. As the fish grow they move downstream, until the onset of adulthood sends the fish on a journey to the ocean. Before life ends, each fish returns to the stream of its birth to renew the cycle and lay its own eggs. New science has shown that the dying salmon provide fertilizer for the forest itself, as salmon remains are carried by bears and floods into the thick of the trees. Salmon was also a staple of the native people's diets, and play significant roles in the mythologies up and down the coast. The salmon tail is shown here, flapping and struggling upstream, bringing its beauty and vitality to an otherwise simple vest. Closed with a brooch, it will become a wardrobe staple for three seasons.

Designed by Terri Shea

Skill level
Easy to Intermediate

Size
S (M, L, XL)

Finished Measurements
Bust: 33 (35½, 39, 42½, 44½)" (83.8 [90.2, 99, 108, 113]cm)
Length: 23 (24, 24, 26, 26)" (58.4 [61, 61, 66, 66]cm)

Materials
- 738 (738, 861, 984, 1107) yd. (675 [675, 788, 900, 1013]m) of any DK or sport weight wool that knits up with the appropriate gauge

Sample knit with: KnitPicks *Swish DK* (100 percent superwash merino wool, 123 yd. [112.5m] per 1¾ oz. [50g] ball): color Terra Cotta, 6 (6, 7, 8, 9) balls

- US size 5 (3.75mm) circular needle, 32" (81.cm) long, *or size to obtain gauge*
- US size 3 (3.25mm) circular needle, 32" (81cm) long
- US size 3 (3.25mm) double-pointed needles
- 6 stitch markers
- Stitch holders or waste yarn
- Tapestry needle

Gauge
24 sts and 32 rows = 4" (10cm) in St st with larger needle

Pattern Stitches

Fishtail Lace

Worked over 17 sts on a background of St st.

Row 1 (RS): K1, YO, k3, ssk, p5, k2tog, k3, YO, k1.

Row 2: P6, k5, p6.

Row 3: K2, YO, k3, ssk, p3, k2tog, k3, YO, k2.

Row 4: P7, k3, p7.

Row 5: K3, YO, k3, ssk, p1, k2tog, k3, YO, k3.

Row 6: P8, k1, p8.

Row 7: K4, YO, k3, sk2p, k3, YO, k4.

Row 8: Purl all sts.

Rep rows 1–8 for patt.

Moss Stitch

Worked over an even number of sts.

Row 1 (WS): *K1, p1; repeat from * to end of row.

Row 2: Knit the knit stitches and purl the purl stitches as they appear.

Row 3: *P1, k1; repeat from * to end of row.

Row 4: Knit the knit stitches and purl the purl stitches as they appear.

Rep rows 1–4 for patt.

Stockinette Stitch (St st)

Row 1 (RS): Knit.

Row 2: Purl.

Rep rows 1 and 2 for patt.

Instructions

Note The vest is worked in one piece and then split into Fronts and Back at the armholes. The stitches not in use can be slipped onto a stitch holder or waste yarn. Each section is then worked separately. V-neck shaping is worked to the inside of the lace pattern.

Lower Body

Using smaller circular needle, cast on 196 (213, 234, 256, 268) sts.

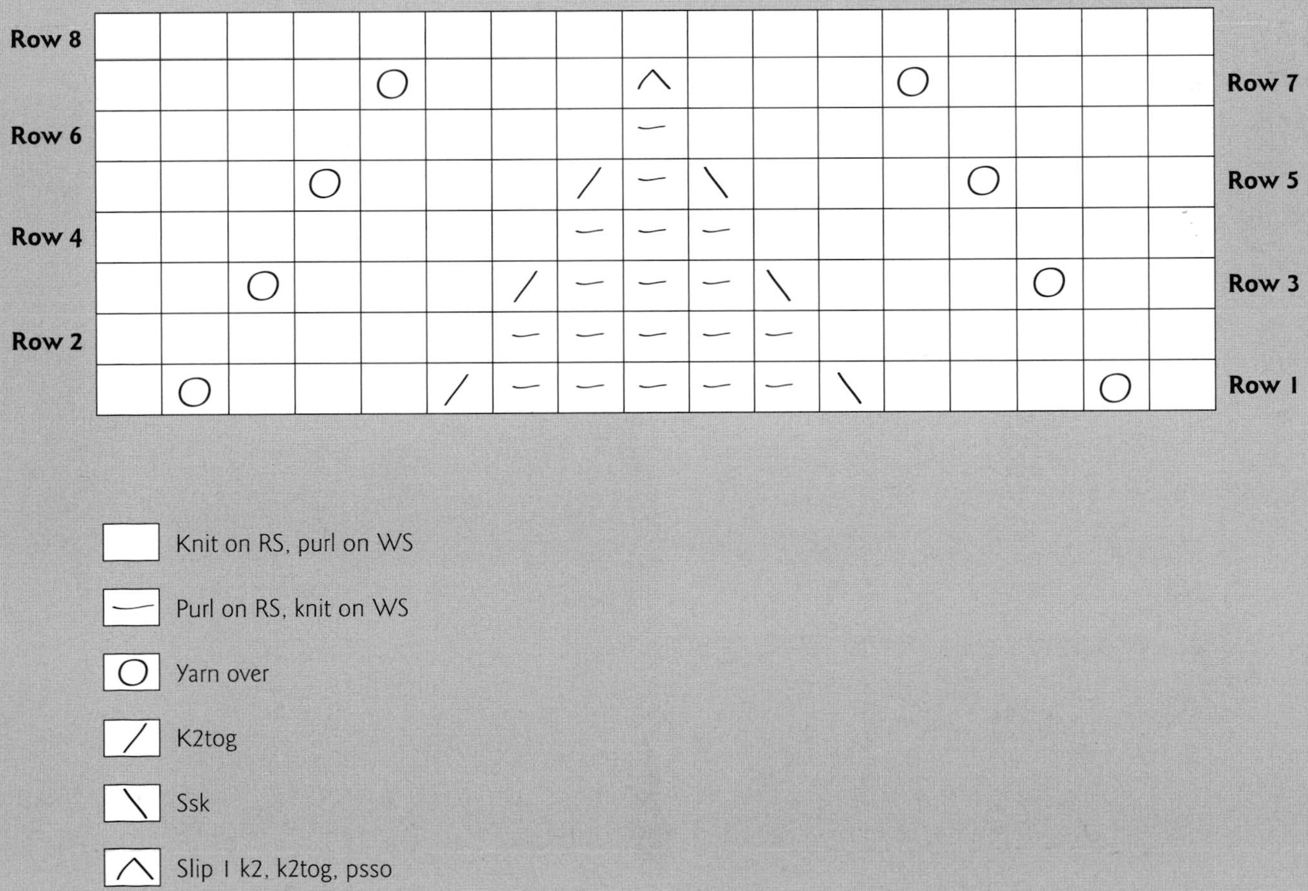

																		Row 8
				O				∧				O						Row 7
								—										Row 6
			O				/	—	\					O				Row 5
							—	—	—									Row 4
		O				/	—	—	—	\					O			Row 3
						—	—	—	—									Row 2
	O				/	—	—	—	—	—	\					O		Row 1

Row 8 — Row 7 — Row 6 — Row 5 — Row 4 — Row 3 — Row 2 — Row 1 *(row labels as marked on chart left and right)*

☐	Knit on RS, purl on WS
—	Purl on RS, knit on WS
O	Yarn over
/	K2tog
\	Ssk
∧	Slip 1 k2, k2tog, psso

Work in moss stitch for 8 rows. Change to larger needles and purl 1 row. Beg Fishtail Lace and stockinette stitch on the next row as follows:

Next row (RS): K2, pm, work row 1 of Fishtail Lace, pm, knit to last 19 sts, pm, work row 1 of Fishtail Lace, pm, k2.

Work in St st with Fishtail Lace inserts at both edges of the piece as established until the lower body measures 5 (5½, 6, 6, 6)" (12.7 [14, 15.2, 15.2, 15.2]cm), ending with a WS row.

Begin Waist Shaping

Next row (RS): Work across 46 (50, 56, 61, 64) sts, ssk, k1, pm for side seam, k1, k2tog, work across 92 (101, 110, 122, 128) sts, ssk, k1, pm for side seam, k1, k2tog, work across rem 46 (50, 56, 61, 64) sts—4 sts decreased, 192 (209, 230, 252, 264) sts rem.

Decrease on either side of these side markers every 6 rows 2 more times—184 (201, 222, 244, 256) sts rem.

Work 8 rows even.

Increase every 6 rows on either side of the side markers 3 times—196 (213, 234, 256, 268) sts.

Work as established until piece measures 13 (14, 14, 15, 15)" (33 [35.6, 35.6, 38.1, 38.1]cm).

Shape V-Neck

Next row (RS): Work 20 sts as established, k2tog, work to 3 sts before last marker, ssk, work as est to end of row—194 (211, 232, 254, 266) sts rem.

Decrease at neck edge in this manner every 4 rows 2 (2, 2, 4, 4) more times, ending after a WS row—46 (50, 56, 59, 62) sts rem in each Front portion and 98 (107, 116, 128, 134) in the center Back portion, for a total of 190 (207, 228, 246, 258) sts. Lower body should measure approx 14 (15, 15, 17, 17)" (35.6 [38.1, 38.1, 43, 43.2]cm).

Right Front

At this time you will separate the Right Front from the work, decrease for the arm hole, and continue shaping V-Neck.

With RS facing, put all sts after the first side seam marker on hold to work Back and Left Front later.

Working on the 46 (50, 56, 59, 62) Right Front sts only, on RS rows, continue working Fishtail Lace between the markers while continuing to dec at the neck edge every

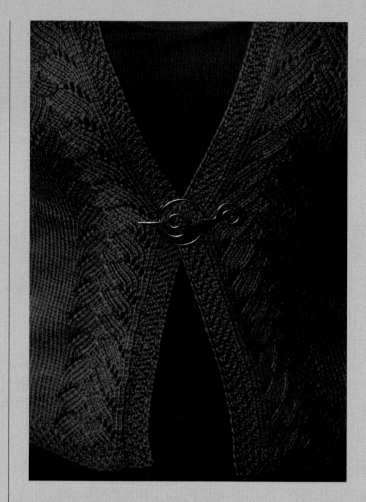

4 rows another 14 (16, 19, 17, 19) times and *at the same time,* begin armhole shaping as follows.

Shape Armhole

On WS rows, bind off armhole in 6 steps as follows:

Row 1 (WS): Bind off 5 (5, 5, 7, 7) stitches, work to end of row as est.

Row 2 (and all RS rows): Work as est and dec at neck edge as noted above.

Row 3: Bind off 2 (3, 3, 4, 4) stitches, work to end of row as est.

Row 5: Bind off 1 (2, 2, 3, 3) stitches, work to end of row as est.

Row 7: Bind off 1 (1, 2, 2, 2) stitches, work to end of row as est.

Row 9: Bind off 1 (1, 1, 1, 1) stitches, work to end of row as est.

Row 11: Bind off 0 (0, 1, 1, 1) stitches, work to end of row as est.

Work until armhole 8 (8½, 8½, 8½, 9)" (20 [21.5, 21.5, 21.5, 23]cm) from the first bound-off sts and dec at neck edge until 22 (22, 23, 24, 25) sts rem. Bind off.

Back

Slip 98 (107, 116, 128, 134) sts onto larger needles.

Working in St st, bind off 5 (5, 5, 7, 7) sts at beg of next 2 rows.

Bind off 2 (3, 3, 4, 4) sts at beg of next 2 rows.

Bind off 1 (2, 2, 3, 3) sts at beg of next 2 rows.

Bind off 1 (1, 2, 2, 2) sts at beg of next 2 rows.

Bind off 1 (1, 1, 1, 1) st at beginning of next 2 rows.

Bind off 0 (0, 1, 1, 1) sts at beginning of next 2 rows—78 (83, 88, 92, 98) sts rem.

Continue in St st until Back measures 7½ (7½, 7½, 7½, 8)" (19 [19, 19, 19, 20]cm). Place stitch markers over center 17 sts and work 1 rep of Fishtail Lace.

Continue in St st until Upper Back measures 8 (8½, 8½, 8½, 9)" (20 [21.5, 21.5, 21.5, 23]cm) and matches Right Front. Bind off all sts.

Left Front

Slip rem 46 (50, 56, 59, 62) Left Front sts from holder onto larger needles. Left Front is worked as a mirror Right Front.

On WS rows, continue working Fishtail Lace between the markers while continuing to dec at the neck edge every 4 rows another 14 (16, 19, 17, 19) times and *at the same time,* begin armhole shaping as follows.

Shape Armhole
On RS rows, bind off armhole in 6 steps as follows:

Row 1 (RS): Bind off 5 (5, 5, 7, 7) stitches, work to end of row as est.

Row 2 (and all WS rows): Work as est and dec at neck edge as noted above.

Row 3: Bind off 2 (3, 3, 4, 4) stitches, work to end of row as est.

Row 5: Bind off 1 (2, 2, 3, 3) stitches, work to end of row as est.

Row 7: Bind off 1 (1, 2, 2, 2) stitches, work to end of row as est.

Row 9: Bind off 1 (1, 1, 1, 1) stitches, work to end of row as est.

Row 11: Bind off 0 (0, 1, 1, 1) stitches, work to end of row as est.

Work until armhole measures 8 (8½, 8½, 8½, 9)" (20 [21.5, 21.5, 21.5, 23]cm) from the first bound-off sts and dec at neck edge until 22 (22, 23, 24, 25) sts rem. Bind off.

Finishing

Wash and dry flat to block; take care to flatten fronts so that the lace flows smoothly around the V-neck.

Sew the shoulder seams.

Front Band

Starting at bottom right edge, using smaller circular needle, pick up 2 sts for every 3 rows of knitting on the body (that is, pick up 2, skip 1), pick up 1 st for every bound-off stitch at back neck. You will have approximately 296 (300, 300, 310, 310) sts on the needle. The exact number is not important as long as you are close and you follow the 2-to-3 ratio and have an even number of sts. Work in moss stitch for 7 rnds. Bind off all stitches in patt.

Armhole openings (work both same)

Starting at underarm, using dpns, pick up 108 (112, 112, 112, 120) sts around armhole. Work in moss stitch for 7 rnds. Bind off all stitches in patt.

Steam Front and Armhole edgings.

Designer Bio

Terri Shea is a former web developer who lives and designs knitwear from Seattle, Washington. Terri's designs have been published in magazines such as *Knitter's* and *Cast On;* Knitnet.com, an online magazine; Cherry Tree Hill Yarns and Plymouth Yarns; as well as books such as *Big Girl Knits* (Potter Craft, 2006) and *Rainbow Knits for Kids* (Martingale and Company, 2005). Terri's first book, *Selbuvotter: Biography of a Knitting Tradition* (Spinningwheel Llc, 2007) details the history, techniques, and patterns of Norway's iconic black and white mittens. Read more about Terri's book and Selbu mittens at www.selbuvotter.com.

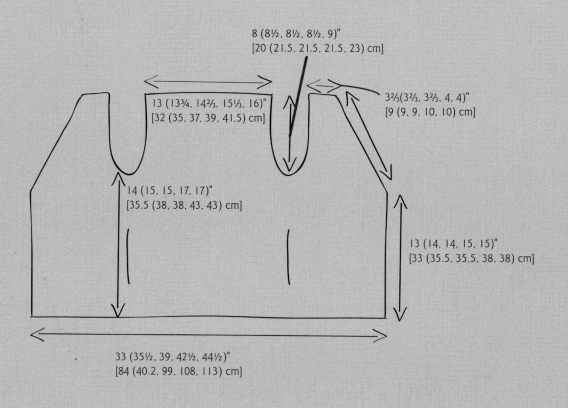

8 (8½, 8½, 8½, 9)"
[20 (21.5, 21.5, 21.5, 23) cm]

13 (13¾, 14⅔, 15⅓, 16)"
[32 (35, 37, 39, 41.5) cm]

3⅔(3⅔, 3⅔, 4, 4)"
[9 (9, 9, 10, 10) cm]

14 (15, 15, 17, 17)"
[35.5 (38, 38, 43, 43) cm]

13 (14, 14, 15, 15)"
[33 (35.5, 35.5, 38, 38) cm]

33 (35½, 39, 42½, 44½)"
[84 (40.2, 99, 108, 113) cm]

Evergreen

This luxuriously oversized stole will keep you warm and cozy on a chilly fall or winter night. Inspired by the lovely evergreen trees in the Pacific Northwest, the pattern is easily memorized and calming to knit.

Designed by Rosemary Hill

Skill level

Intermediate

Size

26 × 98" (66 × 249cm), blocked

Materials

- 1,050 yd. (960m) of any lace weight yarn that knits up with the appropriate gauge

Sample knit with: Madil Kid *Seta* (70 percent kid mohair, 30 percent silk; 230 yd. [210.3m] per 1 oz. [25g] skein): color 432 emerald green, 5 skeins

- US size 8 (5mm) circular needle, at least 24" (61cm) long, *or size to obtain gauge*
- Smooth cotton yarn for provisional cast-on
- 8 stitch markers
- Blocking board (optional) and blocking wires or rust proof pins.

Gauge

17 sts and 18 rows = 4" (10cm) over lace pattern, blocked

Lace Pattern

Row 1 (RS): K5, *p1, YO, (sl 1, k1, psso), k8, k2tog, YO, p1* repeat from * to* 6 more times, k5.

Row 2 (WS): K6, *p1, YO, p2tog, p6, (p1, wyif sl 1 kwise, sl both sts back on left needle, pass sl st over p st, put st on right needle), YO, p1, k2* repeat from *to* 6 more times, k4.

Row 3: K5, *p1, k2, YO, (sl 1, k1, psso), k4, k2tog, YO, k2, p1* repeat from *to* 6 more times, k5.

Row 4: K6, *p3, YO, p2tog, p2, (p1, wyif sl 1 kwise, sl both sts back on left needle, pass sl st over p st, put st on right needle), YO, p3, k2* repeat from *to* 6 more times, k4.

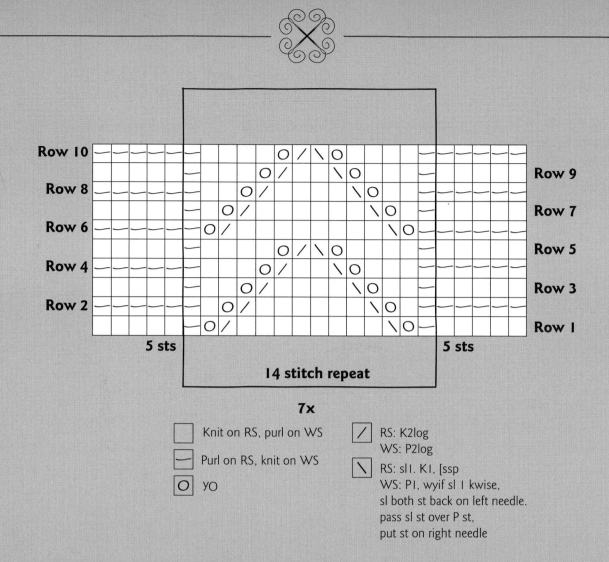

	Knit on RS, purl on WS		/	RS: K2tog WS: P2tog
	Purl on RS, knit on WS		\	RS: sl1. K1, [ssp WS: P1, wyif sl 1 kwise, sl both st back on left needle. pass sl st over P st, put st on right needle
O	YO			

Row 5: K5, *p1, k4, YO, (sl 1, k1, psso), k2tog, YO, k4, p1* repeat from *to* 6 more times, k5.

Row 6: K6, *YO, p2tog, p8, (p1, wyif sl 1 kwise, sl both sts back on left needle, pass sl st over p st, put st on right needle), YO, k2* repeat from *to* 6 more times, k4.

Row 7: K5, *p1, k1, YO, (sl 1, k1, psso), k6, k2tog, YO, p1* repeat from *to* 6 more times, k5.

Row 8: K6, *p2, YO, p2tog, p4, (p1, wyif sl 1 kwise, sl both sts back on left needle, pass sl st over p st, put st on right needle), YO, p2, k2* repeat from *to* 6 more times, k4.

Row 9: K5, *p1, k3, YO, (sl 1, k1, psso), k2, k2tog, YO, k3, p1* repeat from *to* 6 more times, k5.

Row 10: K6, *p4, YO, p2tog, (p1, wyif sl 1 kwise, sl both sts back on left needle, pass sl st over p st, put st on right needle), YO, p4, k2* repeat from *to* 6 more times, k4.

Rep rows 1–10 for patt.

Instructions

Note *After you work a few rows of the lace pattern, attach a safety pin to mark the right side.*

Using waste yarn, provisionally cast on 108 sts.

Knit 15 rows.

Work all rows or lace chart 40 times, placing markers between repeats.

Knit 15 rows.

Bind off using picot bind-off as follows: *CO 2 sts using knitted cast on; k2tog tbl, k1 tbl, pass first st worked over second as if binding off, bind off 2 sts, sl st from right needle back to left needle*; rep from * to * to end of row.

Pick up sts from provisional cast-on and bind off using the same picot bind-off.

Finishing

Weave in ends and wet block using blocking wires.

98" (259cm)

26" (66cm)

Designer Bio

Rosemary Hill, a northern California native, was taught by her grandmother to crochet at the age of four. Beading, knitting, drawing, and painting followed. Despite attempts to become a musician, Ms. Hill succumbed to her love of visual arts and founded a graphic design studio with her husband, a photographer. While pregnant with her second child, she began knitting again after a long hiatus.

Learning to knit lace prompted the founding of her company, Designs by Romi (www.designsbyromi.com), selling handmade shawl pins and sweater closures. In 2006, she began designing knit jewelry and lace. Her patterns have appeared in *Knitty*, an online magazine, and her first book, *Elements of Style: Creating Jewelry with Wire, Fiber, Felt, and Beads* was published by Interweave Press in 2008.

ESTES PARK

chapter 10
Estes Park
Wool Market

The Estes Park Wool Market isn't the largest festival in terms of vendors, or in terms of sheep competition events. While it's very well attended, it's not anything like the size of Maryland Sheep and Wool. This is what all the Colorado knitters say when I ask them about their local festival. They make it seem as though, really, Estes Park is just a nice regional market, good for meeting up with their friends and for a day out. They all say, well, it's fun for us, but probably it's not anything special.

They are wrong. First, there's the setting to consider. As I come into town, I see two elk bathing in Estes Lake, just next door to the municipal dog park and Stanley Park Fairgrounds. These sites are framed against a backdrop of stunning mountains that surround the town. Estes Park, situated in a natural valley, is also the historic entrance to Rocky Mountain National Park. Meet up with a friend for an elk, buffalo, or venison burger lunch here, and she'll tell you about the bighorn sheep that she saw along the highway on her drive into town.

OK, Coloradans might say, we've got the scenery going for us . . . but that's not all. On the Friday before the festival, the fairgrounds begin to fill up with paco-vicuñas—a fawn- to cinnamon-colored alpaca and vicuña crossbred animal shown for the first time in Colorado. These animals, bred from wild South American vicuñas for their softness, fineness, rarity, and color, share the alpaca's domesticated ease of handling, longer fiber, and denser fleece. While the vicuñas themselves are not exported to the United States, their crossbred offspring are, and there are a lot of them now in Colorado.

Just after seeing these exotic creatures and determining they are the highlight of the festival, I pass the yaks. There are two yaks on display, and neither is the typical chocolate brown seen in spinning fiber sold in the United States. One is black, and the other, a white and black mixture. Both yaks sidle up to the fence to have their foreheads scratched. To my surprise, these yaks on display have outgoing personalities.

Then there are the Cashmere goats. There's a breeder who sits in a camping chair in the middle of her pen in the goat tent, where Angoras and Pygoras also share the limelight. She's cleaning up her goat kids for the Cashmere goat show on Sunday. The goat, slung across her lap like a large dog, looks comforted and safe as she carefully brushes out wood shavings and other detritus. Lee Hawkins explains that as the goats age, they become too big for this and she combs them on a stand to harvest the precious cashmere fiber rather than on her lap. Other than that, the process is the same!

Meanwhile, nearby, a high school kid says when she tells her classmates that she raises fiber animals, some look puzzled at her hobby. Others, including her teachers, share her passion and gossip about goats in Colorado's rich fiber animal community. How weird is it, she wonders, when her teachers approach and ask if they might buy one of her goats!?

Next, there's an alpaca fleece show that more than wows the average spinner. The prizewinning fleeces compete in fineness with those paco-vicuñas, and the colors range from jet black to charcoal, to fawn and white. All the while, I pass llamas and their owners as they go to compete in obstacle courses and other events in the competition ring. These are not just your every day llamas. I see a variety of llamas with long flowing curls. Their Suri locks resemble Suri alpacas, only the animals are twice as large. There are llamas that seem like they're "on steroids" towering above us, larger than any llamas I've seen before.

The sheep tent is small, and even shares space with Angora rabbits. Yet, one can see everything from Shetlands and Jacobs sheep to Karakuls, Teeswaters, and Wensleydale in the rare breed department, and I'm stunned by the sheer size of the Rambouillet, California Variegated Mutant (CVM) cross, and Corriedales on display. While locals in their understated way seem to think these are run-of-the-mill sheep, I know different. They grow their sheep big in the West!

None of this should overshadow the vendors' barn, where there's buffalo yarn and fiber, yak down, and fine raw fleeces so clean that you wonder if they've already

One of High Prairie's yaks visits with Devlin Anderson.

It's hard to imagine competing against these beautiful (and large) llamas.

been washed. Knitters are bombarded with color and luxury, with hand-spun, hand-dyed and hand-painted yarns both local and exotic. There are pelts to purchase, gorgeous thick Swedish Lovikka mittens, and even sheep skin slippers for everyone, toddler to adult. I'm stopped dead in my tracks by Elsa Sheep and Wool Company's naturally colored Cormo garments and the yarns, spun in every yarn weight from lace weight to worsted. More clever yet, Elsa has some of the Cormo fine wool flock's yarn spun woolen for extra loft, softness, and warmth, and some spun worsted, for a smoother, denser, yarn that drapes and wears well.

While I make my purchases, desperate for more Cormo fine wool, bloggers meet and greet at pre-arranged places outside in the bright spring weather, hugging and chatting about their purchases. They're bubbly with a day well spent.

Maybe it's the 8,000-foot altitude and I'm lightheaded, or the sunburn and dehydration from a day out in high elevation sunshine, but I don't think Estes Park Wool Market is "no big deal." When I leave these fairgrounds, I'm deeply envious of Colorado's premier fiber festival. I wonder if Colorado locals are understated about their incredible scenery and amazing yearly event for good reason. If they keep saying it's "nothing special," maybe it won't get too crowded. Maybe those of us from out of state won't come and ruin their good time. Even as I write this, I wonder if I should delete all the special bits, and help Coloradans keep their secret, the Estes Park Wool Market, in all its exotic and native wonder.

Mountain Ripple Socks

These socks are quick and easy to make and look lacy and elegant on the feet. Hand-painted yarn works well for this pattern and re-creates the colors and terrain of the Colorado Rockies. The length of the sock and ripples can be adjusted to fit perfectly.

Designed by Cathy Adair-Clark

Skill level

Intermediate

Size

Women's shoe size 7–10

Finished Measurements

Approx 6¾" (17.1cm) circumference, unstretched

Note Will stretch to fit a foot up to 8½" (21.6cm) in circumference

Materials

- 430 yd. (394m) fine or fingering weight yarn that crochets up at the appropriate gauge

Sample crocheted with: Brown Sheep *Wildfoote Luxury Sock Yarn* (75 percent washable wool, 25 percent nylon; 215 yd. [197m] per 1¾ oz. [50g] skein): color Lilac Desert, 2 skeins

- Size D crochet hook, *or size to obtain gauge*
- Stitch markers

Gauge

7 sc and 7 rows = 1" (2.5cm)

6 dc (or ½ a ripple patt) and 2 rows = 1" (2.5cm)

Special Stitches

2-sc dec (2 single crochet decrease)
Insert hook in next st, pull up loop, insert hook in next st, pull up loop, YO, pull through all loops on hook.

2-dc dec (2 double crochet decrease)
YO, insert hook into next st, pull up loop (3 loops on hook), insert hook in next st, pull up loop (4 loops on

hook), YO and pull through 3 loops, YO and pull through last 2 loops on the hook.

3-dc dec (3 double crochet decrease)
YO, insert hook into first st, pull up loop (2 loops on hook), insert hook into next st, pull up loop (3 loops on hook), insert hook into next st, pull up loop (4 loops on hook), YO pull thru 3 loops (3 loops left on hook), YO, pull loop thru last 3 loops on hook (1 loop left on hook).

Instructions

Note You will work thru both loops on the tops of the crochet sts. You will not ch 1 at the beginning of sc rows or sl st into the last sc. This makes a continuous sc fabric without seams for the toes.

Toe

Make a slip knot and ch 10.

Rnd 1: Sc in second ch from hook, sc across row to last ch, 3 scs in last ch, sc in next sc (working in bottom of ch), sc across row to last sc, 2 sc in last sc—20 sc.

Place marker in last sc. This will be the indicator for one side of the sock as well as indicator for end of rnds.

Rnd 2: 2 sc in first sc, sc in next 9 sc, 2 sc in next sc (this will be the opposite side of sock—you may add a marker to this side, remembering the original marker indicates the end of the rnds), sc in next 9 sc, 2 sc in last st—22 sc.

Rnd 3: Sc in each sc around.

Rnd 4: Work 1 sc at marker, 2 sc in next sc, sc in next 8 sc, 2 sc in next sc, sc in next sc, 2 sc in next sc, sc in next 8 sc, 2 sc in next sc—26 sc.

Move markers to the sc between the first 2-sc inc on each side.

Rnd 5: Sc in each sc around.

Rnd 6: 2 sc in first sc, sc in next 12 sc, 2 sc in next sc, sc in next 12 sc—28 sc.

Move markers to the first sc of the 2-sc inc.

Rnd 7: Sc in next sc (place marker), 2 sc in next sc, sc in next 11 sc, 2 sc in next sc, sc in next sc, 2 sc in next sc, sc in next 11 sc, 2 sc in last sc—32 sc.

Markers should be between the sets of 2-sc increases on each side.

Rnd 8: Sc in each sc around.

Rnd 9: 2 sc in first sc, sc in next 15 sc, 2 sc in next sc, sc in next 15 sc—34 sc.

Rnd 10: Sc in each sc around to last sc, 2 sc in last sc.

Rnd 11: Sc in first sc, 2 sc in next sc, sc in next 16 sc, 2 sc in next sc, sc in next sc, 2 sc in next sc, sc in each sc to marker—38 sc.

Rnd 12: Sc in each sc around.

Adjust markers so they are at each side of the toe, with 19 sc between each marker. Sc across to first marker.

Sole and Instep

Begin sole and instep (ripple) patts—you will alternate rows (for the soles) and rnds (for the soles and the ripple patt across the top) You are crocheting the soles in sc and the tops in double ripple patt simultaneously.

Row 1 (WS): Sc across 19 sc (ignoring the rem 19 sts which will be the instep), ch 1.

Row 2 (RS): Turn, rep row 1.

Rnd 3 (RS): Do not turn work, begin ripple patt on next 19 instep sts that were not crocheted in rows 1 and 2 as follows: 2-dc dec over first 2 sc, dc in next 2 sc, 3 dc in next sc, dc in next 3 sc, 3-dc dec in next 3 sc, dc in next 3 sc, 3 dc in next sc, dc in next 2 sc, 2-dc dec over next 2 sc (foundation ripple row completed), sc across the next 19 sc (sole); turn.

Row 4: Ch 1, sc across 19 sole sc (ignoring the instep ripple patt); turn.

Row 5: Rep row 4.

Rnd 6: Rep row 4 until you reach end of sc, then follow ripple patt: 2-dc dec in first 2 dc, dc in next 2 dc, 3 dc in next dc (center dc of inc made on rnd 3), dc in next 3 dc, 3-dc decrease in next 3 dc, dc in next 3 dc, 3 dc in next dc, dc in next 2 dc, 2 dc-dec in the last 2 dc. You should be at the beginning of the round.

Note There will be 2 "peaks" and 3 "valleys" of the ripple patt. You will always work 2-dc dec at the ends of the ripple patt and 3-dc dec in the middle.

Rep rows/rnds 4–6 until there are 13 ripple rows.

Heel

You will work only in the sc patt on the sole.

Sc across the sole 19 scs back and forth for 5 rows until sc sole reaches the back of the heel. The sole of the sock from toe to heel should measure 9" [22.9cm] for women's medium-length foot. Try sock on and adjust sole length as necessary by repeating the sc rows across the sole.

Decreasing heel flap

Rnd 1: 2-sc dec in next 2 sc, sc in next 4 sc, 2-sc dec in next 2 sc, sc in next 4 sc, 2-sc dec in next 2 sc, sc in next 3 sc, 2-sc dec in last 2 scs, ch 1, turn—15 sc rem.

Rnd 2: 2-sc dec in first 2 sc, sc across to last 2 sc, 2-sc dec in last 2 sc, ch 1, turn—13 sc rem.

Rnd 3: 2-sc dec in first 2 sc, sc in next 4 sc, 2-sc dec in next 2 sc, sc in next 3 sc, 2-sc dec in last 2 sc, do not turn—10 sc rem.

Place marker at the edge of the heel. This will indicate the end of a rnd.

Leg

Begin ripple patt as follows:

Rnd 1: Ch 2, 2-dc increase in last sc, then crochet 3 dc evenly on the side of the sc sole rows, work 3-dc dec (taking 2 st from edge row at side of heel and next 1 dc from the previous ripple row), follow ripple patt across top of foot, 3 dc-dec (last 1 dc and 2 st from edge row), work 3 dc evenly across sc edges at opposite side of heel, 3 dc in the corner, dc in next 3 sc, 3-dc dec, dc in next 3 sc, sl st in top of ch-2.

Rnd 2: Ch 2, dc in next 2 dc *3-dc dec, dc in next 3 dcs, 3-dc in next dc, dc in next 3 dcs* 3 times, 3-dc dec, dc in next 3 dcs, 3 dc in last dc. Sl st on top of ch-2.

Rnds 3–6: Work ripple patt evenly as established.

Try on the sock.

If the sock fits fine, continue the ripple patt for 6 more rnds or until the height desired.

Finishing

Edging: *Sc, ch 1; rep from * to end of rnd.

Fasten off. Weave in ends.

Follow yarn label washing instructions.

Designer Bio

Cathy Adair-Clark has been crocheting, spinning, and knitting for more than half her life. She blogs at www.catena.typepad.com.

Men's Crochet Mock Cable Sweater

At every festival, there are men wearing stunning handmade sweaters to fend off the early morning chill in barns and on the fairgrounds. The ingenious pattern of this mock cable sweater changes all the standard assumptions about crochet. It's a gorgeous crocheted creation with just a touch of knitted ribbing, made with a wool and alpaca blend that offers a warm, hardwearing and handsome appeal. Ideal for a casual evening out or those early mornings in the Rockies, these mock cables are tempting enough that you can bet there will be a lot of women borrowing this new wardrobe classic . . . or making it for themselves.

Designed by Kim Guzman

Skill level

Intermediate

Sizes

S (M, L, XL, XXL, XXXL)

Finished Measurements

Finished Chest: 39 (43, 48, 52, 56, 60)" (99 [109, 122, 132, 142, 152.5]cm)

To Fit Chest Sizes: 36 (40, 44, 48, 52, 56)" (91.5 [102, 112, 122, 132, 142]cm).

The sample is made in size M.

Materials

- 1,790 (1,980; 2,180; 2,400; 2,640; 2,900) yd. (1,640 [1,815; 1,995; 2,195; 2,415; 2,655]m) of any DK weight yarn that works up at the appropriate gauge

Sample was made with: Green Mountain Spinnery *Alpaca Elegance* (50 percent fine wool, 50 percent alpaca; 180 yd. [164m] per 2 oz. [56g] skein): color Cappuccino, 10 (11, 13, 14, 15, 17) skeins

- US size I (5.5mm) crochet hook, *or size to obtain crochet gauge*
- US size 8 (5mm) straight knitting needles, *or size to obtain knit gauge*
- US size 7 (4.5mm) circular knitting needle, 16" (41cm) long for neckband
- 1 split-ring stitch marker
- Tapestry needle
- 1 round stitch marker

Gauge

15 sts and 17 rows = 4" (10cm) in mock cable stitch

18 sts and 26 rows =4" (10cm) in K2, P2 ribbing

Special Stitches

Short Single Crochet (ssc): Insert hook from bottom to top under the horizontal bar below the front loop of the single crochet, YO and pull up a loop. YO and pull through 2 loops.

Decrease Single Crochet (dec sc): Insert hook into st indicated, YO and pull up a loop. Insert hook into next st, YO and pull up a loop. YO and pull through 3 loops.

Extended Single Crochet (esc): Insert hook into st indicated, YO and pull up a loop. YO and pull through one loop. YO and pull through 2 loops.

Mock Cable Stitch

Note *The number of back loop single crochets worked at the end of row 4 will vary according to the location in the garment. This row is of primary concern in maintaining the stitch pattern throughout. Be careful to line up the double crochets throughout the garment to keep the stitch pattern continuous.*

Ch indicated number.

Foundation row (RS): Sc in second ch from hook and in each rem ch, ch 1; turn.

Row 1 (WS): Ssc in each sc across, ch 1; turn.

Row 2: Working in BL only, sc in each sc, ch 1; turn.

Row 3: Ssc in each sc across. ch 1; turn.

Row 4: * Working in BL only, sc in next 4 sc, dc in both lps of sc 4 rows below; rep from * across, ch 1; turn.

Rows 5 and 6: Ssc in each st across, ch 1; turn.

Repeat rows 1–6 for patt.

The ribbing is not shown in the schematic measurements

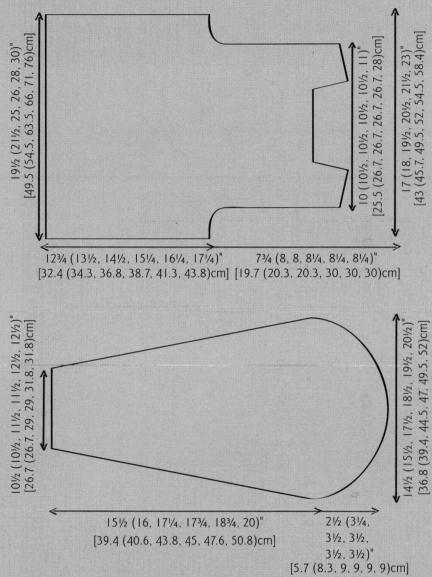

19½ (21½, 25, 26, 28, 30)" [49.5 (54.5, 63.5, 66, 71, 76)cm]

10 (10½, 10½, 10½, 10½, 11)" [25.5 (26.7, 26.7, 26.7, 26.7, 28)cm]

17 (18, 19½, 20½, 21½, 23)" [43 (45.7, 49.5, 52, 54.5, 58.4)cm]

12¾ (13½, 14½, 15¼, 16¼, 17¼)" [32.4 (34.3, 36.8, 38.7, 41.3, 43.8)cm]

7¾ (8, 8, 8¼, 8¼, 8¼)" [19.7 (20.3, 20.3, 30, 30, 30)cm]

10½ (10½, 11½, 11½, 12½, 12½)" [26.7 (26.7, 29, 29, 31.8, 31.8)cm]

14½ (15½, 17½, 18½, 19½, 20½)" [36.8 (39.4, 44.5, 47, 49.5, 52)cm]

15½ (16, 17¼, 17¾, 18¾, 20)" [39.4 (40.6, 43.8, 45, 47.6, 50.8)cm]

2½ (3¼, 3½, 3½, 3½, 3½)" [5.7 (8.3, 9, 9, 9, 9)cm]

Instructions

Note When working a row of sts in 1 loop only, always work the last st of the row in both loops for stability.

Back

Back is worked vertically, from side to side. Maintain the st patt throughout.

Make a slip knot and ch 50 (53, 57, 60, 64, 67).

Foundation row: Sc in second ch and in each rem ch across, ch 1; turn—49 (52, 56, 59, 63, 66) sc.

Work even in mock cable stitch, beg with row 1 of patt, until 4 (6, 8, 8, 10, 12) rows have been completed from beg, not counting foundation chain. At end of final row, ch 2, turn.

Armhole Shaping

Next row: Sc in second ch from hook and work mock cable stitch across, ch 1; turn—50 (53, 57, 60, 64, 67) sts.

Next row: Work in patt to last st, work 2 sc in last st—51 (54, 58, 61, 65, 68) sts.

Sizes L, XL, XXL and XXXL only: Ch 2, turn, then rep previous 2 rows once more—60 (63, 67, 70) sts.

At end of final row, ch 28 (29, 27, 28, 27, 28), turn.

Next row: With split-ring stitch marker, mark the first st of this row as the top. Sc in second ch from hook, work in mock cable stitch across, ch 1; turn—78 (82, 86, 90, 93, 97) sts.

Work even in mock cable stitch until 9 (13, 17, 19, 21, 23) rows have been completed from beg.

Shoulder Shaping

Next row: Work mock cable stitch to last st, work 2 sc in last st, ch 1; turn—79 (83, 87, 91, 94, 98) sts.

Next row: Work even in mock cable stitch, ch 1; turn.

Rep previous 2 rows once more—80 (84, 88, 92, 95, 99) sts.

Work even until 21 (25, 31, 35, 39, 43) rows have been completed from beg.

Neckline Shaping

Next row: Work in mock cable stitch to last 2 sts, dec sc across last 2 sts, ch 1; turn—79 (83, 87, 91, 94, 98) sts.

Next row: Dec sc across first 2 sts, work in mock cable stitch across, ch 1; turn—78 (82, 86, 90, 93, 97) sts.

Rep previous 2 rows until a total of 27 (31, 37, 41, 45, 49) rows have been completed from beg—74 (78, 82, 86, 89, 93) sts after final row.

Work even until 61 (67, 73, 77, 81, 87) rows have been completed from beg.

Next row: Work in mock cable stitch to last st, work 2 sc in last st, ch 2, turn—75 (79, 83, 87, 90, 94) sts.

Next row: Sc in second ch from hook, work in mock cable stitch across, ch 1; turn—76 (80, 84, 88, 91, 95) sts.

Rep previous 2 rows until 67 (73, 79, 83, 87, 93) rows have been completed from beg—80 (84, 88, 92, 95, 99) sts on final row.

Work even until 76 (82, 90, 96, 102, 110) rows have been completed from beg.

Opposite Shoulder Shaping

Next row: Dec sc across first 2 sts, work in patt across, ch 1; turn—79 (83, 87, 91, 94, 98) sts.

Next row: Work even, ch 1; turn.

Rep previous 2 rows once more—78 (82, 86, 90, 93, 97) sts.

Work even until 81 (89, 97, 105, 111, 119) rows have been completed from beg.

Opposite Armhole Shaping

Next row: Work across 51 (54, 60, 63, 67, 70) sts only, ch 1; turn, leaving rem sts unworked.

Next row: Dec sc across first 2 sts, work across each rem st, ch 1; turn—50 (53, 59, 62, 66, 69) sts.

Next row: Work even to last 2 sts, dec sc across last 2 sts, ch 1; turn—49 (52, 58, 61, 65, 68) sts.

Sizes L, XL, XXL and XXXL only: Rep previous 2 rows once more—56 (59, 63, 66) sts.

Work even until 87 (97, 109, 117, 125, 135) rows have been completed from beg. Fasten off.

Ribbing

With straight knitting needle and RS facing, pick up 88 (96, 108, 116, 124, 136) sts across bottom edge, turn.

Row 1: (K2, p2) to end of row.

Row 2: Knit the knit sts and purl the purl sts.

Rep row 2 until ribbing measures approximately 3" (7.6 cm). Bind off all sts.

Front

Front is worked vertically, from side to side. Maintain the st patt throughout.

Work as for the Back until 21 (25, 31, 35, 39, 43) rows have been completed from beg.

Neckline Shaping

Next row: Work across 72 (76, 78, 82, 83, 87) sts only, ch 1; turn, leaving rem sts unworked.

Next row: Dec sc across first 2 sts, work in patt across, ch 1; turn—71 (75, 77, 81, 82, 86) sts.

Next row: Work to last 2 sts, dec sc across last 2 sts, ch 1; turn—70 (74, 76, 80, 81, 85) sts.

Rep previous 2 rows once more—68 (72, 74, 78, 79, 83) sts.

Work even until 29 (33, 39, 43, 47, 51) rows have been completed from beg.

Next row: Work to last 2 sts, dec sc across last 2 sts, ch 1; turn—67 (71, 73, 77, 78, 82) sts.

Work even until 58 (64, 70, 74, 78, 84) rows have been completed from beg. At end of final row, ch 2, turn.

Next row: Sc in second ch from hook and work in mock cable stitch across, ch 1; turn—68 (72, 74, 78, 79, 83) sts.

Work even until 62 (68, 74, 78, 82, 88) rows have been completed from beg. At end of final row, ch 2, turn.

Next row: Sc in second ch from hook and work mock cable stitch across, ch 1; turn—69 (73, 75, 79, 80, 84) sts.

Next row: Work to last st, work 2 sc in last st, ch 2, turn—70 (74, 76, 80, 81, 85) sts.

Rep previous 2 rows once more, at end of final row, ch 9 (9, 11, 11, 13, 13); turn—72 (76, 78, 82, 83, 87) sts, not counting ch.

Next row: Sc in second ch from hook, work in mock cable patt in each rem ch and st across, ch 1; turn—80 (84, 88, 92, 95, 99) sts.

Work even until 76 (82, 90, 96, 102, 110) rows have been completed from beg.

Continue as for Back, starting with Opposite Shoulder Shaping.

Sleeves (Make 2)

Sleeves are worked vertically, from side to side. Maintain the st patt throughout.

Make a slip knot and Ch 5 (16, 12, 6, 10, 6).

Foundation row: Sc in second ch from hook and in each rem ch across, ch 6 (5, 5, 5, 5, 5), turn—4 (15, 11, 5, 9, 5) sc.

Row 1: Sc in second ch from hook and in each rem ch across, work across beginning with Row 1 of mock cable stitch each rem st to last sc, work 2 sc in last sc, ch 1, turn—10 (20, 16, 10, 14, 10) sts. With split-ring stitch marker, mark the last st of this row as the top of the sleeve.

Row 2: Work in mock cable stitch to last st, esc in last st, [Esc in 2 bottom legs of previous st] 4 (3, 3, 3, 3, 3) times, sc in 2 bottom legs of previous st, ch 6 (5, 5, 5, 5, 5) times; turn—15 (24, 20, 14, 18, 14) sts.

Row 3: Sc in second ch from hook and in each rem ch across, work across each rem st to last sc, work 2 sc in last sc, ch 1; turn—21 (29, 25, 19, 23, 19) sts.

Rep previous 2 rows until 10 (12, 14, 16, 16, 18) rows have been completed from beg—54 (65, 70, 73, 77, 82) sts on final row.

Next row: Work even, ch 1; turn.

Next row: Work to last st, work 2 sc in last st, ch 1, turn—55 (66, 71, 74, 78, 83) sts.

Rep previous 2 rows until 22 (26, 30, 30, 30, 30) rows have been completed from beg—60 (72, 78, 80, 84, 88) sts on final row.

Work even until 44 (46, 50, 54, 58, 62) rows have been completed from beg.

Next row (RS): Dec sc across first 2 sts, work across each rem st, ch 1; turn—59 (71, 77, 79, 83, 87) sts.

Next row: Work even, ch 1; turn.

Rep previous 2 rows until 56 (60, 66, 68, 72, 74) rows have been completed from beg—54 (65, 70, 73, 77, 82) sts on final row.

Next row: Dec sc across first 2 sts, work across to within last 5 (4, 4, 4, 4, 4) sc, ch 1; turn, leaving rem sts unworked—48 (60, 65, 68, 72, 77) sts.

Next row: Sl st across 5 (4, 4, 4, 4, 4) sts, work in mock cable stitch across each rem st, ch 1; turn—43 (56, 61, 64, 68, 73) sts.

Rep previous 2 rows until 65 (71, 79, 83, 87, 91) rows have been completed from beg—4 (15, 11, 5, 9, 5) sts on final row.

Next row: Work even.

Fasten off.

Ribbing

With straight knitting needle and RS facing, pick up 48 (48, 52, 52, 56, 56) sts across bottom edge.

Row 1 (WS): (K2, p2) to end of row.

Row 2: Knit the knit sts and purl the purl sts.

Rep Row 2 until Ribbing measures approximately 2½" (6.4cm). Bind off all sts.

Finishing

Set in sleeves. Sew sides and underarm seams.

Neckband

With circular knitting needle and RS facing, starting at left shoulder, pick up 112 (116, 120, 120, 124, 124) sts evenly around neck. Begin working in the rnd.

Rnd 1: (K2, p2) to end of rnd.

Rnd 2: Knit the knit sts and purl the purl sts.

Rep row 2 until Neckband measures approx 1½" (3.8cm).

Bind off all sts. Weave in all ends carefully.

Designer Bio

Kim Guzman has been crocheting and designing for over 30 years. Kim began working as a freelance designer almost a decade ago. Since then, she's sold approximately 250 crochet, knit, and latch hook designs. Her last crochet pattern leaflet sold out of its first printing in just over 5 months. Read more information on her popular website, www.crochetkim.com, which boasts 3 million visitors since its inception.

chapter 11
The Wool Festival at Taos

The Wool Festival at Taos isn't just a weekend event. It's a state of mind. People who want the full experience come several days early, signing up to take courses on Navajo spinning and weaving in the classic Rio Grande (Hispanic) Southwest traditions. Others come just to explore the incredible riches of an area that is full of fiber art year-round. The first weekend in October, the town of Taos is flooded with tourists who have wool on the brain.

The festival's premise is a special one. Twenty-some years ago, the festival was just one day and people sold their wares from the back of their pickups. Decorations came complete with cattle skulls to help draw people in. Yet, from the very beginning, the goal of the Mountain and Valley Wool Association (MVWA) remained focused. This, according to the official Wool Festival at Taos program, is a "producer/fiber artist association, dedicated to the promotion of our regional fibers." Nearly every vendor comes from New Mexico, Colorado, and Texas, and all vendors help make the Wool Festival a reality. That vibrant and strong community is evident throughout the event. While other fiber festivals may have vendors from all over the country, the Wool Festival at Taos celebrates the strong fiber arts tradition of their area by limiting vendors from outside the region.

Bright strong sunshine, blue skies with puffy clouds, and a typically perfect high-desert day make the festival a dependable success. Kit Carson Park is filled with festival participants and vendors, and the setup is symbolic. Each

Lisa de Burlo's hand-spun and dyed fleece–spun yarn sparkles in the sun.

numbered stall lines up to make the outline of a plaza or town square. In the center, the sight and smell of cooked lamb and other foods lure people in to eat lunch. As well, there are tents for demonstrations and a competitive wool show and hand-spun yarn and garment show. On the second day of the festival, the vendors all contribute their wares to a silent auction, which draws support for the MVWA. On the outskirts of the square, there's a stage for blade and electric sheep shearing demonstrations, and a small animal display. A block from the historic Taos Plaza, the MVWA establishes its own temporary settlement. The crowds fill this new square, reveling in the fiber arts community that Taos and New Mexico have made.

What a town it is, too. Filled to the brim with vibrant colors, produced from traditional natural dyes, I am buffeted by the high desert wind from booth to booth. Each booth in the square seems more amazing than the next. In some, traditional Navajo looms, weavings, and spindles were for sale. In others, artists such as Liesel Orend of Earth Arts and Fred Black of Big Sage Architects combine traditional methods with a modern approach, weaving works of art, complete with new symbolism. Liesel Orend's booth showed both old and new, with a hand-woven saddle rug woven in an old Spanish pattern called "the Dazzler," with purple and blue, framed in white that rippled in the light, and a completely modern interpretation of Aphrodite, not just the goddess of love, but also the bee goddess, with both six bees and six hexagonal honeycombs woven in the piece.

This mixture of old and new carries over in every direction with a vengeance. Lisa de Burlo, of Lisa Joyce Designs, sold only two things in her booth, and the booth's design won first place at the festival in 2007. Original handmade felted wool hats from U. S. wool tempted those who wanted an artsy finished product. Her hand-spun "fleece-spun" yarns, spun exclusively from Black Pines Sheep's Wensleydale/Lincoln fleeces, titillated the senses of everyone else. All these bulky textured yarns, curly with sheep's locks, are spun by Lisa by hand on a Rio Grande spinning wheel in a traditional South-western approach to spinning—in the grease (without washing the wool first). Then, Lisa dyes them outdoors in an astonishing array of colors. This is the quintessential novelty yarn for the natural fibers enthusiast.

Locally produced natural fibers represent the core of this event: alpaca, llama, cashmere, buffalo, Angora rabbit and mohair, as well as an inspiring array of fine wools such as California Variegated Mutant (CVM), Australian Bond, and the old standbys Merino, Rambouillet, Cormo,

New Mexico Weaving Traditions

In an area of rich fiber arts traditions, one can't pretend that the Wool Festival is the only thing to see. If you're coming north from Albuquerque or Santa Fe take the High Road to Taos. On the way, stop at the Espanola Valley Fiber Arts Center to see a nonprofit cooperative at work. You can purchase a ball of yarn or two, weave on one of the many looms, or visit with other fiber artists at work. Pick up a New Mexico Fiber Arts Trails brochure or booklet. Don't hesitate to wander off the beaten track to see these weavers.

The drive up to Taos goes through Chimayo, an important historic center for Classic Rio Grande (Hispanic) weaving. Defined by the early Spanish settlers, these weavers often use a stand-up walking loom, also known as a Rio Grande, as compared to the Anglo floor loom, where one weaves while seated. Many weavers in this region win national awards for their work and families are known for their multiple generations of skilled weavers. In particular, don't miss Centinela Traditional Arts, The studio and gallery, where Irvin Trujillo, recent National Heritage Fellowship Award winner and seventh generation weaver, works with his wife, accomplished spinner and weaver, Lisa Trujillo. Mr. Trujillo's work is on permanent display in the Museum of American History in Washington, D.C.

Other fiber arts traditions go back even farther in New Mexico's history. When passing the multiple pueblos along the way to the festival, imagine the Indians who've created hand-spun cotton and plant textiles since 800 CE on both backstrap and vertical looms. (A *backstrap* loom is an ancient form of traditional weaving. One end of the weaving is tied to a fixed object like a door or post, and the other end is strapped around one's back.)

A Chimayo loom.

The Navajo developed a special weaving tradition, based on their religion and culture. According to the *Dineh* (the name the Navajo use to represent their people), they learned to weave and tend sheep from the Spider Woman, who first wove her web of the universe and taught the Navajo. Many rich colors in their rugs traditionally came from local natural dyes, and indigo originally brought by the Spaniards. The bright red sometimes came from unraveled serapes and trade blankets brought to the area by outsiders. Now, the Navajo use a variety of dyes and resources to continue their weaving tradition. Most Navajo looms are portable, rectangular, and vertical, made out of simple materials. Sitting on rugs that can be adjusted in height, the Navajo loom allows the weaver to see all of her work, as compared to other looms, which require the weaver to roll up finished fabric in order to continue weaving.

Today, there are both modern and traditional weavers whose work shows the influence of all these weaving traditions. As you visit each studio or vendor's stall, don't forget to ask about a weaver's materials, preferred loom, and designs. That conversation is likely to be as varied and inspirational as the weavings themselves.

The Trujillo family's naturally dyed yarns dry in the sun.

and Corriedale are for sale. Still, in New Mexico, the traditional Navajo-Churro wool remains king, as it has for the last 400 years.

Everyone learns something new throughout the day. Shearing demonstrations show off Navajo-Churro lambs, also for sale at the event. The animals on display show passersby what this important breed looks like, as well as Mount D'oro, another regional breed. Sharon White, in her 70s, demonstrates blade shearing on her Mount D'oro sheep, explaining that she still shears her 40 sheep and some of her neighbors' flocks this way. A few alpacas, Pygora goats, and Angora rabbits dot the landscape, and leashed working dogs parade the grounds, from the sheep-guarding Great Pyrenees to the herding border collies.

At the demonstration tent, knowledgeable people field questions from attendees. Want to learn how a Colorado fiber mill produces its special fine fiber blends? Linda Dewey, Lonesome Stone Natural Fiber Mill's owner, offers details on how to select the right fleeces and blends, and how to skirt them yourself. Need to know how to use a certain kind of loom or spindle? Every vendor at this event is knowledgeable and happy to share.

Wander outside of the park's perimeter to the adobe buildings of Taos and you don't leave any of the artistry behind. Festival goers naturally want to see La Lana Wools, a nationally known yarn shop close by which features hand-dyed, hand-spun yarns year-round, available at the shop or online.

Walk a block further to see Rachel Brown's creation, Weaving Southwest. This shop, half gallery and half spinning and weaving supply, shows the wide range of modern fiber artistry. In the front of the store, striking modern rugs and tapestries vie for attention. The Rio Grande Wheel, a great wheel with a spindle that still allows the spinner to treadle sitting down, is sold here and thus the store is a famous stop for curious spinners. (This wheel is great for creating bulky novelty yarns, such as the ones sold by Lisa Joyce Designs.) Venture further to see the store's line of dyed knitting yarns, Navajo-Churro rug yarns, and see both tapestry and Rio Grande looms for sale, which require a weaver to work standing up.

Sharon White blade shears one of her Mount D'oro sheep.

Continue through the town and notice the looms and spinning wheels for sale at other shops, or stop to see more at the local weaving studios. Just a bit further up the road in Arroyo Seco, the Taos Sunflower yarn shop entertains the festival overflow with fabulous sales on a lovely selection of unique and sustainable yarns. The festival is a great excuse to visit Taos, but fiber arts are center stage year-round.

Navajo-Churro Sheep

The Navajo-Churro sheep is a Southwestern tradition. Brought to the area by the Spanish in the 1500s, this sheep breed has been nurtured by the Navajo for over 400 years, even through U. S. government–sanctioned slaughter (called *stock reduction*), wars, droughts and relocations. Despite numerous attempts by outsiders to "improve" the breed, the arid environment and isolated communities helped to preserve this rare breed of sheep to do what it does best—produce Navajo and classic Rio Grande (Hispanic) rugs. The Navajo-Churro is a hardy, small animal with what looks like a shaggy coat. Some may have two or four horns, and others may be *polled*—meaning without horns. Raised mostly for their wool, the Navajo-Churro's hardwearing fiber is versatile for the handspinner and weaver, as the sheep produce a wide diversity of natural colors.

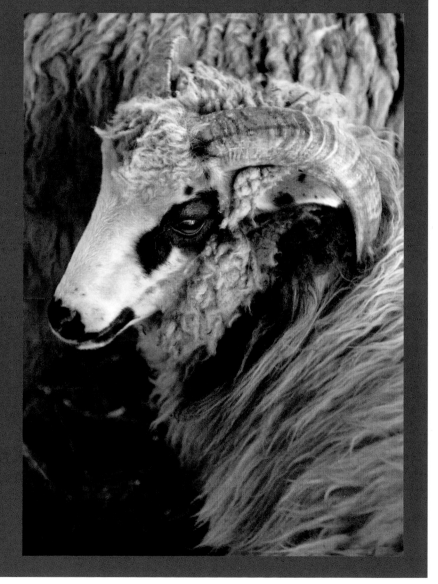

Today, Navajo, Hispanic, and Anglo weavers in New Mexico all rely on this unique local wool, found in most stalls at the festival. Spinning it is easy, with its low grease content and coarse and open lock structure. While commercially spun and dyed Navajo-Churro is now available, many weavers still rely on some version of the old techniques, spinning yarn on a Hispanic *malacate* (thigh spindle), Navajo spindle, or on a variety of spinning wheels. The rugs, saddle bags, and blankets traditionally produced with this wool have myriad uses and are still prevalent throughout New Mexico. The thick clay walls of adobe houses in the Southwest can be cold in the winter. What better insulator is there than a rug or blanket, handwoven from local sheep in the traditional way?

A Trio of Southwestern-Style Pillows

The Southwest is filled with light, colors, and unique textiles. These pillows, while each is a distinct piece of art, share geometric forms as well as the intense hues of La Lana wools' naturally dyed fiber. Knit one or three to transport yourself to Taos and its festival.

Designed by Judy Dercum

Skill level

Intermediate with Intarsia knitting skills required

Size

All pillows: 16" (40.5cm) square

Canyon Echoes Pillow

The Canyon Echoes design was inspired by the beautiful sandstone walls of Canyon De Chelly National Monument in the Navajo Nation Reservation. The Walnut, Kota, *or* Navajo Tea *in the "Te Rosata," and Indian Paintbrush are all traditional native dyes that match the landscape of the Southwest. The intarsia technique enables the stepped block motif to be used. The color blocks are large so the intarsia is easy to knit.*

Canyon Echoes, Navajo Footsteps, and Ancient Memories pillows.

Materials

- 200 yd. (183m) each of tan (MC) and brown (CC I), and 210 yd. (192m) of variegated brown/red (CC II) bulky weight yarn that knits up with the appropriate gauge

Sample knit with:

MC: La Lana Wools *Knitting Worsted Millspun* (100 percent fine wool; 200 yd. [183m] per 4 oz. [113g] skein): color Indian Paintbrush, 1 skein

CC I: La Lana *Knitting Worsted Millspun* (100 percent fine wool; 200 yd. [183m] per 4 oz. [113g] skein): color Dark Walnut, 1 skein

CC II: La Lana Wools *Forever Random Worsted Mohair Accents* (66 percent Romney wool, 33 percent yearling mohair; 70 yd. [64m] per 2 oz. [56.7g] skein): color Te Rosata, 3 skeins

Navajo Footsteps Pillow

This pillow has the traditional stepped motif of the native culture of Southwestern America. The black and red colors are traditional Navajo rug colors, and the variegated yarn allows the finished pillow to fit in many color schemes. It is fun to knit using the intarsia technique and the finished product is small enough to be carried along in a knitting bag. Best of all, the results are beautiful!

Materials

- 200 yd. (183m) of black (MC), 210 yd. (192m) of variegated red (CC I), and 70 yd. (64m) of multicolored (CC II) bulky weight yarn that knits up with the appropriate gauge

Sample knit with:

MC: La Lana Wools *Knitting Worsted Millspun Black* (100 percent fine wool; 200 yd. [183m] per 4 oz. [113g] skein): color Hand-Dyed Black, 1 skein

CC I: La Lana Wools *Forever Random Worsted* (100 percent Romney wool; 210 yd. [192m] per 6 oz. [170g] skein): color Potpourri, 1 skein

CC II: La Lana Wools *Forever Random Worsted Obverse* (60 percent Romney wool, 40 percent yearling mohair; 70 yd. [64m] per 2 oz. [56.7g] skein): color Tzarina, 1 skein

Ancient Memories Pillow

The soft colors of this pillow remind me of the evening sunsets, Southwestern mesas, and the delicate flowers of the springtime desert landscape. Take this project along on a drive through the Painted Desert in Arizona!

Materials

- 200 yd. (183m) tan, 140 yd. (128m) variegated peach, and 140 yd. (128m) variegated orange bulky weight yarn that knits up with the appropriate gauge

Sample knit with:

MC: La Lana *Knitting Worsted Millspun* (100 percent fine wool; 200 yd. [183m] per 4 oz. [113g] skein): color Indian Paintbrush, 1 skein

CC I: La Lana Wools *Forever Random Worsted Glace* (60 percent yearling mohair, 40 percent Romney wool; 70 yd. [64m] per 2 oz. [56.7g] skein): color Peach Perfect, 2 skeins

CC II: La Lana Wools *Forever Random Worsted Obverse* (60 percent Romney wool, 40 percent yearling mohair; 70 yd. [64m] per 2 oz. [56.7g] skein): color Sweet Lorraine, 2 skeins

Other Materials for All Pillows

- US size 8 (5mm) straight needles or circular needle *or size to obtain gauge.*
- Bobbins or small plastic bags (optional)
- US size E-4 (3.5mm) crochet hook
- Tapestry needle
- 16 × 16" (40.5 × 40.5cm) pillow form
- Blocking wires (optional)

Select either a closure with a zipper or a closure with buttons.

If Using a Zipper Closure

- 14" (35.5cm) zipper
- Sewing needle, matching thread, and contrasting thread

If Using a Button Closure

- Five ¾" (2cm) buttons
- Sewing needle and matching thread

Gauge

14 sts and 20 rows = 4" (10cm) in St st

Stockinette Stitch

Row 1 (RS): Knit.

Row 2 (WS): Purl.

Repeat rows 1 and 2 for patt.

Intarsia Technique

Intarsia is a type of knitting with several colors worked in blocks. It is worked flat, usually in St st. The fabric is a single thickness, unlike stranded knitting that is double or triple thickness depending on how many colors are used. Use separate balls of yarn for each color block. Use bobbins or make butterflies to hold the yarn. Small plastic bags can be used to hold the different colors.

- **Beginning a new color:** Insert the right needle into the next st. Place the end of the new color between the tops of the needles and across the old color from left to right. Pick up the new color under the old color and work the next st. Then, move the tail of the new color off the right needle. Carry the tail along the back, twisting it in as you work the sts with the new color.

- **Changing colors:** Twist the new color yarn around the old color yarn at each color change to avoid making holes. Whether knitting or purling, the new color yarn is to the right of the old color yarn. Drop the old color yarn and with your right hand, reach under it for the new color. Twist in as many ends as possible while knitting.

- **Carrying yarn:** It may be necessary to carry yarn along to a new starting point. To carry the yarn to the left, take the unused yarn across the back of the work, twisting it around the working yarn every few sts to the point where it will be used.

If there will be a **color offset that will move to the right on the next row,** carry the yarn that will be needed along on the wrong side and twist it in with the working yarn to the point where it will be needed. On the next row, it will be in the right position to be used.

Note *If you have forgotten to do that, insert the right needle into the stitch where the new color begins, and place the offset yarn across the back and under the working yarn. Work the stitch with the carried new color yarn. The new yarn will be tied in and stranded across the back. On a knit row, work in the stranded yarn along the back by inserting the tip of the right needle into the next stitch, and then down to pull up the loop. Knit the stitch, at the same time dropping the loop. Do not knit the loop. Then work the next stitch. This can be repeated until the strand is secure, while working the new block.*

Knitting in the strand is not absolutely necessary because the inside of the pillow will not be subject to snagging. Sew in any ends that have not been knit in.

Reading Charts

The charts are 50 sts wide by 76 rows high. They are read from bottom to top, right to left for right side rows (odd rows, knit), and left to right for wrong side rows (even rows, purl). Each square represents a knitting stitch.

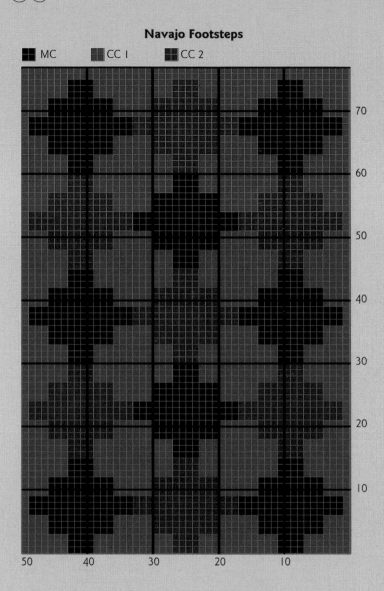

Navajo Footsteps

■ MC   ■ CC 1   ■ CC 2

Instructions for All Pillows

Make butterflies or use bobbins or small plastic bags to hold small amounts of each color of yarn.

Back

With MC, cast on 50 sts.

Beg chart working in St st, working back and forth. When the last row (76) of the chart has been completed, bind off with MC.

Using MC and crochet hook, finish all edges as follows:

Rnd 1: Work 50 sc along each edge, plus 1 ch to turn each corner, sl st to first sc after making ch at fourth corner.

Rnd 2: Ch 1, do not turn, work around edge of pillow again, working 1 sc into each sc, plus 1 ch to turn each corner, sl st to first sc after making ch at fourth corner. Pull yarn through the last loop to fasten off.

Front

With MC, cast on 50 sts.

Beg chart working in St st, working back and forth. When the last row (76) of the chart has been completed, select the style of closure and follow the appropriate finishing instructions.

Finishing

Zipper Closure

With MC, bind off all sts.

Using MC and crochet hook, finish all edges with 2 rnds of sc as for Back.

Wet block pieces taking care to make them square and the correct size, 16 × 16" (40.5 × 40.5cm). Using blocking wires ensures straight edges.

Lay the Front and Back top edges of pillow pieces together so the edges touch (side by side) with RS facing up. Place the zipper underneath. Pin 1" (2.5cm) from each end, and then baste in place with contrasting sewing thread. Make sure the zipper lines up perfectly. With matching thread, backstitch the zipper to the WS at the edges. Be sure the sewing doesn't show on the RS. Then, on the RS, sew the crochet edge close to the zipper with stitches that don't show but catch any loose yarn. Remove the basting thread.

Canyon Echoes

MC CC 1 CC 2

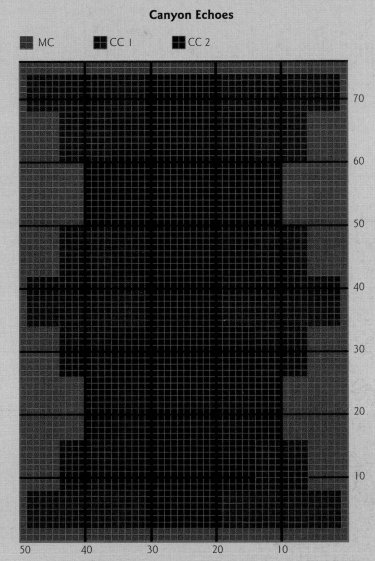

Place the pillow pieces with WS together, and sew the remaining 3 edges together with mattress stitch, using a tapestry needle and MC yarn. Be sure to secure the seam at the ends of the zipper. Sew in any loose ends and insert the pillow form.

Button Closure

Do not bind off after finishing chart.

Flap: Using MC, purl one RS row to form extension turn line. Continue in St st for 2" (5cm) after turn line, ending with a RS row. Knit 4 rows. Bind off all sts.

Wet block pieces taking care to make them square and the correct size, 16 × 16" (40.5 × 40.5cm) for back and 16 × 19" (40.5 × 45.6cm) for back. Using blocking wires ensures straight edges.

Fold flap to inside and sew together along side edges with MC and tapestry needle.

Using MC and crochet hook, finish all edges with 2 rnds of sc as for Back, stopping before completing second rnd on the top edge (fourth side).

Along top edge (fourth side), make 5 evenly spaced buttonholes along edge by making one ch for each st you're skipping for the desired length of the buttonhole and continue in patt as established. Finish by pulling yarn through the last loop.

Place the two pillow pieces together, WS facing. Sew three sides tog with mattress stitch, excluding the opening edge, with a tapestry needle and MC. Using sewing thread, sew on buttons to back edge of front pillow piece opposite the buttonholes on the back piece. Sew in any loose ends.

Place the pillow form into the pillow with the top edge under the flap at the top of the front piece. Button the pillow together and sit back and enjoy!

Designer Bio

Judy Dercum is a knitwear designer and teacher whose specialty is color and its use in intarsia, slip stitch mosaic, and stranded knitting techniques. Her designs are influenced by the landscape and colors of the American Southwest. Her work has appeared in several books, including: *Knitting in America* (Artisan, 1996), *Knitter's Stash* (Interweave Press, 2001), *Handpaint Country* (XRX Books, 2002), *Simple Knits for Sophisticated Living* (Quarry Books, 2003), and *The Natural Knitter* (Potter Craft, 2007) as well as in magazines such as *Interweave Knits*, *Knitter's*, and *InKnitters*. She is a featured designer for La Lana Wools of Taos, New Mexico.

Ancient Memories

MC CC 1 CC 2

chapter 12
Conclusions: Building Your Own Fiber Gathering

Large festivals like Maryland Sheep and Wool or Rhinebeck are special experiences, but they're only one type of fiber gathering. Many of us depend on regular small groups to satisfy our fiber "fix" and to visit with one another, and these, too, are important gatherings. Finding your place in the fiber arts world can take a lifetime of learning. It's better to do that exploration with friends.

In many cities, there are organized guilds with lots of services. When I lived in Buffalo, New York, I joined the Knitters Guild of Greater Buffalo. With evening meetings that feature guest speakers and teachers from the United States, nearby Canada, and beyond, there are sometimes over 100 people in attendance . . . all of them knitting. This is a formal and large guild with satellite meetings, newsletters, guest speakers and events. There are even discounts for members at the many local yarn stores . . . but for me, it provided a weekly afternoon knitting group. I lived in Buffalo for just one year, but the older ladies at

that gathering provided me with the mothering I needed and a warm, smart, and talented knitting crowd. We all need support sometimes, and I found that ready-made group meaningful during a time when I truly lacked community.

Other groups are perhaps less formal, but no less meaningful. In North Carolina, the Twisted Threads Fiber Guild is widely dispersed geographically around the Raleigh area, and has a large online list. In person, these gatherings are smaller, meeting twice a month, usually in people's homes. These meetings, held in living rooms, offer an informal chance to learn, share, and visit with one another. During the four years I spent in Durham, North Carolina, this group allowed me to make lifelong friends, many of whom I saw again while researching this book.

With many shepherds as part of Twisted Threads, it's a special treat to meet on a farm during lambing season. Other members offer visits with Angora rabbits, alpacas, or goats. It's not unusual to purchase homemade cheese, eggs, soaps, or that perfect fleece from a farmer friend at an ordinary meeting. These women are bright and run the gamut from research scientist to fiber business owner to home-schooling mom. As the group is so diverse, it's not uncommon for older members to knit up baby sweaters as presents for a new mother, or for the whole group to participate in creating an afghan for a member undergoing chemotherapy. This kind of group becomes much more than a place to spin or knit.

In the fall of 2006, many in Apex, North Carolina faced an evacuation. A chemical fire with explosions and toxic smoke at a local industrial plant threatened both Twisted Threads Guild members and their animals. The first thing that guild members did after checking on their own safety and that of their livestock was to offer shelter to anyone who had to evacuate. Concerned messages rushed onto the online list, with offers to "just come" if anyone or their animals needed to evacuate. Everyone was safe, and more than one felt grateful for the interlocking network of "twisted threads."

If you're new to this crafty stuff, or moving to a new neighborhood, it can take some work to find these rich pockets of fiber arts. There are lists of festivals, guilds, and other resources on the Web. You can also ask for information about fiber gatherings at your local knitting store. In some places, you may have to build your own!

While starting your own festival might be overwhelming, creating your own small monthly or weekly group isn't. Post signs at your library, local co-op, or grocery store, mention to friends that you're a weaver or spinner, or that you crochet or knit. Sooner or later, you'll find another person with your interests. From there, it's easy to get together for a cup of tea, a visit, and some sharing. Bringing your spinning, weaving, knitting, or other fiber arts pursuits to a public place, like a farmer's market, a local museum, or library, will help entice others to join you. Before you know it, you'll have a community of your own.

Wherever you are, you can create or find your own gathering. Whether your event is a huge festival, small dyeing day for friends, formal guild, or a small informal group is up to you. If you can't manage to travel to the big festivals, give your own neighborhood a chance. Be proud of what you do. I found my favorite local sheep farm—mentioned in the sheep shearing chapter—because I met someone at my husband's faculty "happy hour" who knew I was a spinner. That person just happened to know a retired colleague who kept sheep. I followed up on the lead, and made a friend.

In an urban area, you may not be near sheep farms, but you're likely to find many more yarn shops, knitters, spinners, and other like-minded enthusiasts. Live in a rural setting? Slow down if you happen to see a field of sheep, a llama, or alpaca. Take the time to ask around or jot down the address. Drop that farm a note asking what they do with all that fiber! Visit your local feed store and ask if anyone keeps fiber animals. Look for ways to create the positive adventures and neighborhood cooperation that we all seek at fiber festivals and gatherings.

Everywhere I traveled while researching *Fiber Gathering*, I met people who asked which festival was "the best." One might be able to figure out the biggest festival, or the one that had the most exotic animals, competitive events, classes, or lamb burgers, but that's not what makes a fiber gathering a good time. I could have concocted a complicated ratings scheme to demonstrate all the components that make a fiber arts event a success. The conclusion I came to is far less scientific.

All of these festivals, and the many events I couldn't manage to include, were different, interesting, and "the best." It's all about *the people* who make festivals, state fair competitions, sheep shearings, spinning groups, and knitting guilds possible. It's the vendors, shepherds, 4-H competitors, fellow shoppers and attendees, teachers and demonstrators, pattern designers, sheep-to-shawl participants and their patient partners from Maryland to Oregon and everywhere in between, who are the best. Thank you for making me welcome at your fiber gathering. Thank you for enriching us all with your warmth and community.

Thick & Thin Baby Coat & Cap

Keep the little ones in your life snuggly and warm in this quick and easy cardigan and cap set. The thick-and-thin yarn is easily replaced with your favorite hand-spun and works with the stitch pattern to create an irresistible texture.

Designed by Chrissy Gardiner

Skill level

Easy

Size

6m, 12m, 18m, 2T, 4T

Finished Measurements

Sweater Chest: 19 (20½, 22, 24½, 27)" (48 [52.1, 55.8, 62.3, 68.5]cm)

Hat Circumference: 13¼ (14½, 16, 18½, 20)" (34 [37, 40.5, 47, 51]cm)

Materials

- 290 (345, 390, 480, 585) yd. (265 [315, 357, 440, 535]m) of any bulky weight yarn with the appropriate gauge

Sample knitted with: Lorna's Laces *Revelation* (100 percent wool; 125 yd. [114m] per 4 oz [113g] skein): color 62 Child's Play, 3 (3, 4, 4, 5) skeins

- US size 10 (6mm) straight needles for coat, *or size to obtain gauge*
- US size 8 (5mm) straight needles for ribbing
- Tapestry needle
- 3 buttons, ¾" (19mm) diameter
- Sewing needle and matching thread
- Set of 5 US size 10 (6mm) double-pointed needles for cap, or size to obtain gauge
- Stitch marker

Gauge

12 sts and 20 rows = 4" (10cm) over St st with larger needle

Pattern Stitches

Ridged Rib For Coat

Worked over a multiple of 2 sts + 1.

Row 1 (WS): *P1, k1; repeat from * to last st, p1.

Row 2: Knit the knit sts and purl the purl sts.

Rows 3 and 4: Knit.

Repeat rows 1–4 for patt.

1 × 1 Rib

Worked over a multiple of 2 sts + 1.

Row 1 (WS): *P1, k1; repeat from * to last st, p1.

Row 2: Knit the knit sts and purl the purl sts.

Repeat rows 1 and 2 for patt.

Ridged Rib For Hat

Worked over a multiple of 2 sts.

Rnds 1 and 2: *K1, p1; repeat from * to end.

Rnd 3: Purl.

Rnd 4: Knit.

Repeat rounds 1–4 for patt.

Instructions for Coat

Back

With larger straight needles, cast on 29 (31, 33, 37, 41) sts.

Work in Ridged Rib until the Back measures 9 (9½, 10, 11, 12)" (23 [24, 25.5, 28, 30.5]cm). End after working row 2 of Ridged Rib patt. Bind off all sts.

Right Front

With larger straight needles, cast on 13 (15, 15, 17, 19) sts.

Work in Ridged Rib until the front measures 7 (7½, 8, 9, 10)" (18 [19, 20, 23, 25.5]cm). End after working a WS row.

Right Neck

Next row (RS): Bind off 2 (3, 3, 3, 4) sts, work to end in ridged rib as established.

Next row (WS): Work even in Ridged Rib over remaining 11 (12, 12, 14, 15) sts.

Decrease row: K1, ssk, work to end in Ridged Rib as established—10 (11, 11, 13, 14) sts rem for right shoulder.

Repeat last 2 rows 0 (0, 0, 1, 2) more times—10 (11, 11, 12, 12) sts rem for right shoulder.

Work even in Ridged Rib until the Right Front measures the same as the Back.

Bind off all sts.

Left Front

Work as for Right Front to neckline. End after working a RS row.

Left Neck

Next row (WS): Bind off 2 (3, 3, 3, 4) sts, work to end in Ridged Rib as established.

Decrease row (RS): K1, ssk, work to end in Ridged Rib as established—10 (11, 11, 13, 14) sts rem for left shoulder.

Next row: Work even in Ridged Rib.

Repeat last 2 rows 0 (0, 0, 1, 2) more times—10 (11, 11, 12, 12) sts rem for left shoulder.

Work even in Ridged Rib until the Left Front measures the same as the Back.

Bind off all sts.

Sleeves (make 2)

With larger straight needles, cast on 21 (23, 25, 27, 29) sts.

Work in Ridged Rib for 1" (2.5cm). End after working a WS row.

Increase row (RS): K1, m1, work in Ridged Rib as established to last st, m1, k1.

Work even in Ridged Rib as established, making sure to work increased sts in patt as they are added, for 3 rows.

Repeat the last 4 rows 5 more times—there are now 33 (35, 37, 39, 41) sleeve sts.

Work even until Sleeve measures 6½ (7½, 8, 9, 10½)" (16.5 [19, 20, 23, 26.5]cm). End after working row 2 of ridged rib patt. Bind off all sts.

Pockets (make 2)

With larger straight needles, cast on 9 (11, 11, 13, 15) sts.

Work in 1 × 1 rib for 2¾ (3, 3, 3½, 4)" (7 [7.5, 7.5, 9, 10] cm). Bind off all sts.

Finishing

Sew the shoulder seams, sew the sleeves to the coat body and then sew the underarm seams.

Position pockets on Front of coat approximately 1½" (4cm) from bottom edge of coat and 1" (2.5cm) from unseamed edges of coat Fronts and sew in place.

Thick & Thin Baby Coat & Cap

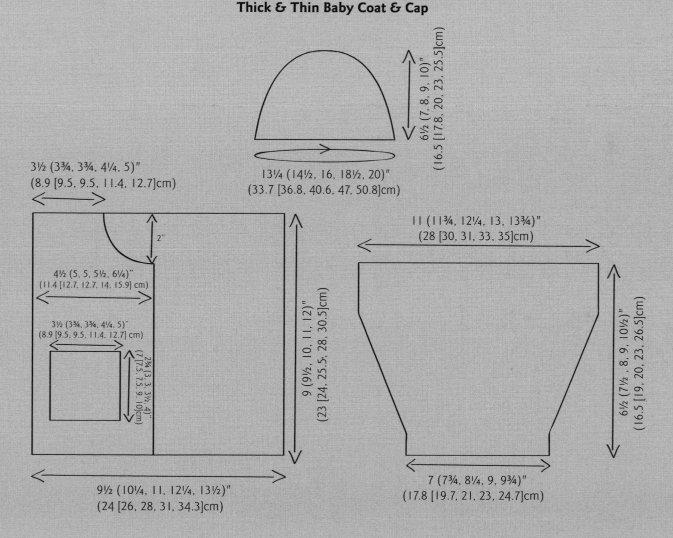

Button Band

Starting at the Right Front neck edge with WS facing, use smaller straight needles to pick up 26 (28, 30, 34, 38) sts evenly down the front of the coat ending at the bottom edge of the Right Front. Work in 1 × 1 rib for 6 rows. Bind off all sts in patt.

Buttonhole Band

Starting at the bottom edge of the Left Front with WS facing, use smaller straight needles to pick up 26 (28, 30, 34, 38) sts evenly up the front of the coat ending at the Left Front neck edge.

Work in 1 × 1 rib for 2 rows.

Next row (RS): Work in 1 × 1 rib for 3 (2, 3, 2, 3) sts, *bind off the next 3 sts, work in 1 × 1 rib for 3 (4, 4, 6, 7) sts; repeat from* 2 more times, bind off the next 3 sts, work to end.

Next row: Work in 1 × 1 rib to first set of bound-off sts, *cast on 3 sts over the sts bound off in the previous row, work in 1 × 1 rib for 3 (4, 4, 6, 7) sts; repeat from* 2 more times, work to end.

Next row: Work in patt. and cast on 3 sts over the sts bound off in the previous row, work to end.

Work in 1 × 1 rib for 2 more rows. Bind off all sts in patt.

Weave in all ends on the WS of the work using a tapestry needle.

Dampen with cool water and lay flat to block.

Position buttons on button band and sew in place using sewing needle and matching thread.

Instructions for Hat

Using double-pointed needles, cast on 40 (44, 48, 56, 60) sts. Join without twisting, place st marker to indicate beginning of rnd and begin working in the round.

Work in Ridged Rib for hat until the hat measures 3½ (4, 5, 6, 7)" (9 [10, 12.5, 15, 18]cm). End after working round 3 of ridged rib patt.

Decrease rnd: *K2, k2tog; repeat from* to end of rnd.

Work rnds 1–3 of Ridged Rib for hat on the remaining 30 (33, 36, 42, 45) sts.

Decrease rnd: *K1, k2tog; repeat from* to end of rnd.

Work rounds 1–3 of Ridged Rib for hat on the remaining 20 (22, 24, 28, 30) sts.

Decrease rnd: *K2tog; repeat from * to end of rnd.

Work rnds 1–3 of Ridged Rib for hat on the remaining 10 (11, 12, 14, 15) sts.

Repeat the last decrease rnd, knitting the extra st leftover at the end of the rnd for the 12m and 4T sizes only—5 (6, 6, 7, 8) sts rem.

Repeat the last decrease rnd once more, knitting the extra st leftover at the end of the rnd for the 6m and 2T sizes only—3 (3, 3, 4, 4) sts rem.

Finishing

Break yarn leaving a 6" (15cm) tail. Thread the yarn tail through the remaining sts using a tapestry needle. Pull tight to close the hole in the top of the hat and secure by weaving in the yarn tail on the wrong side of the work.

Weave in all other ends on WS of the work using a tapestry needle.

Dampen with cool water and lay flat to block.

Designer Bio

Chrissy Gardiner is a mom of two small children and knitwear designer in beautiful Portland, Oregon, where she is lucky to be in close proximity to several great fiber festivals each year. You can see more of her work in various books, magazines and at www.gardineryarnworks.com.

Classy Aran Long Skirt

Enjoy wearing this long Aran knit wool skirt to help keep you warm on cold winter days. The vertical lines really flatter a shapely figure, and the pattern will keep you engaged. The skirt is knit from the bottom up so that the cables will look correct as they are worked. Knit in two pieces with the cable patterns on the front and seed stitch on the back guarantees that you won't sit down and flatten the cables. No worries about your figure, because these vertical cable panels are very slimming, with a large cable panel up the center front with two smaller cables on either side, each separated by seed stitch panels. These cable panels stay the same throughout the skirt, while only the stitches in the seed stitch panels are decreased for shaping.

Designed by Shirley MacNulty

Skill level

Intermediate

Size

XS (S, M, L, XL)

Finished Measurements

Waist: 23 (25, 27, 30, 33)" (59 [64, 69, 76, 84]cm)

Hip: 33 (35, 37, 40, 43)" (84 [89, 94, 102, 109]cm)

Bottom Width: 47½ (52¼, 55½, 59½, 62¾)" (121 [133, 141, 151, 159]cm)

Length: 31 (32, 33, 34, 35)" (79 [81, 84, 86, 89]cm)

Note *The skirt is fairly heavy and will probably grow a few inches in length when being worn; therefore, plan the finished skirt to be an inch or so shorter than you really want.*

Materials

- 1,494 (1,577; 1,660; 1,743; 1,826) yd. (1,368 [1,520; 1,520; 1,672; 1,672]m) of any medium weight yarn that knits up at the appropriate gauge

Sample knit with: Moda Dea *Washable Wool* yarn (100 percent superwash wool, 166 yd. [152m] per 3½ oz. [100g] ball): color 4413 Ivory, 9 (10, 10, 11, 11) balls

- US size 5 (3.75mm) circular needle, 32" (81cm) long *or size to obtain gauge in Seed St for size XS only*

- US size 7 (4.5mm) circular needle, 32" (81cm) long *or size to obtain gauge in Large Cable pattern St for size XS only*

- US size 6 (4mm) circular needle, 32" (81cm) long *or size to obtain gauge in Seed St for sizes S, M, L and XL*

- US size 8 (5mm) circular needle, 32" (81cm) long *or size to obtain gauge in Large Cable pattern St for sizes S, M, L and XL*

- Cable needle

- 10 stitch markers

- Row counter (optional)

- Tapestry needle

- ¾" (19mm) wide nonroll elastic, 2" (5cm) longer than actual waist measurement

- Large safety pin

- Sewing needle and matching thread

Gauge

21 sts and 38 rows = 4" (10cm) in seed st with US size 5 needle for size XS

23 sts and 34 rows = 4" (10cm) in large cable patt with US size 7 needle for size XS

19 sts and 36 rows = 4" (10cm) in seed st with US size 6 needle for sizes S, M, L, and XL

21 sts and 32 rows = 4" (10cm) in large cable pattern with US size 8 needle for sizes S, M, L, and XL

Special Abbreviations

Ssp (slip, slip, purl 2 together): Wyif slip the next 2 sts as if to knit, 1 at a time, to the right needle. Slip them back to the left needle, 1 at a time, in this same position, purl them together through the back loops.

C4F (cable 4 front): Sl the next 2 sts to the cable needle and hold in front of the work, knit the next 2 sts from the left needle, then knit the 2 sts from the cable needle (slants to the left).

C4B (cable 4 back): Sl the next 2 sts to cable needle and hold in the back of the work, knit the next 2 sts from the left needle, then knit the 2 sts from the cable needle (slants to the right).

T3F (twist 3 front): Sl the next 2 sts to the cable needle and hold in the front of the work, purl the next st from the left needle, then knit the 2 sts from the cable needle (slants to the left).

T3B (twist 3 back): Sl the next st to the cable needle and hold in the back of the work, knit the next 2 sts from the left needle, then purl the st from the cable needle (slants to the right).

Pattern Stitches

Seed Stitch

Worked over any number of sts.

Row 1: *K1, p1; repeat from * to end of row when working with an even number of sts or *k1, p1; repeat from * across row until last st, k1, when working with an odd number of sts.

Row 2 and subsequent rows: Knit the purl sts and purl the knit sts.

Seed Stich

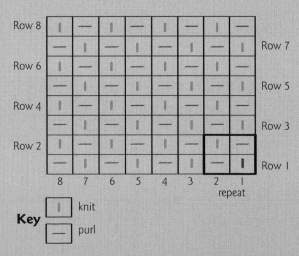

Key | knit — purl

Large Cable Pattern Stitch

24-row patt worked on a multiple of 8 + 4 sts.

Row 1 (RS): P3, *T3F, T3B, p2; repeat from * until 1 st before marker, p1.

Row 2: K4, *p4, k4; repeat from * until marker.

Row 3: P4, *C4F, p4; repeat from * until marker

Row 4: Rep row 2.

Row 5: P3, *T3B, T3F, p2; repeat from * until 1 st before marker, p1.

Row 6: K3, *p2, k2; repeat from * until 1 st before marker, k1.

Row 7: Rep row 1.

Row 8: Rep row 2.

Row 9: Rep row 3.

Row 10: Rep row 2.

Row 11: Rep row 5.

Row 12: Rep row 6.

Row 13: P2 *T3B, p2, T3F; repeat from * until 2 sts before marker, p2.

Row 14: K2, p2 *k4, p4; repeat from * until 8 sts before marker, k4, p2, k2.

Row 15: P2, k2 *p4, C4B; repeat from * until 8 sts before marker, p4, k2, p2.

Row 16: Rep row 14.

Row 17: P2, k2, p3, *T3B, T3F, p2; repeat from * until 5 sts before marker, p1, k2, p2.

Row 18: K2, p2, k3, *p2, k2; repeat from * until 5 sts before marker, k1, p2, k2.

Row 19: P2, k2, p3, *T3F, T3B, p2; repeat from * until 5 sts before marker, p1, k2, p2.

Row 20: Rep row 14.

Row 21: Rep row 15.

Row 22: Rep row 14.

Row 23: P2, *T3F, p2, T3B; repeat from * until 2 sts before marker, p2.

Row 24: Repeat row 6.

Rep rows 1–24 for patt.

Legend

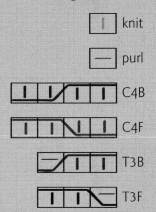

	knit
—	purl
	C4B
	C4F
	T3B
	T3F

Large Cable Pattern

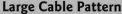

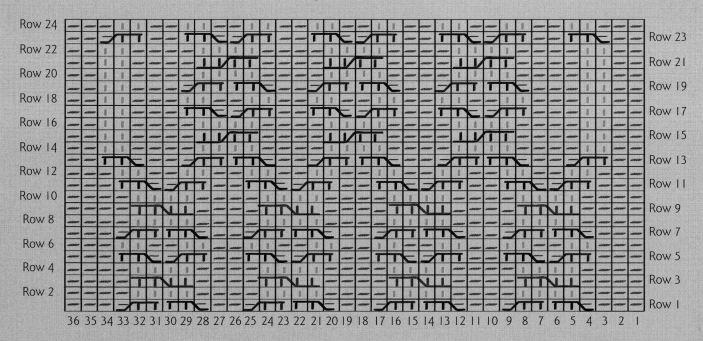

Single Honeycomb

Row 1 (RS): P2, C4B, C4F, p2.

Row 2 (and all WS rows): K2, p8, k2.

Rows 3 and 7: P2, k8, p2.

Row 5: P2, C4F, C4B, p2.

Rep rows 1–8 for patt.

Single Honeycomb

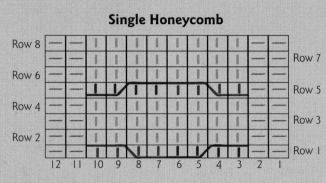

Legend

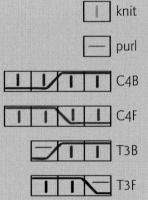

	knit
	purl
	C4B
	C4F
	T3B
	T3F

Claw Stitch

Row 1 (RS): P2, C4B, C4F, p2.

Rows 2 and 4: K2, p8, k2.

Row 3: P2, k8, p2.

Rep rows 1–4 for patt.

Claw Stich

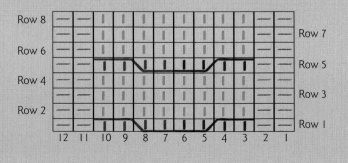

Legend

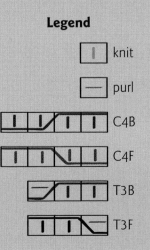

	knit
	purl
	C4B
	C4F
	T3B
	T3F

Instructions

Note *Pieces are worked from lower edge up to waistband.*

Back

Cast on 120 (120, 128, 136, 144) sts with US size 5 (6, 6, 6, 6) needles, using the long-tail cast on.

Begin seed st and work *30 (30, 32, 34, 36) sts, pm, rep from * across row placing markers each time except at the end of row.

Work in seed st for 5 (5, 6, 7, 8)" (12.7 [12.7, 15.2, 17.8, 20.3]cm) slipping markers as you come to them, ending after a WS row.

Back Decrease Rows

First dec row (RS): P1, p2tog, *work in seed st to 2 sts before first marker, ssp, sm, p2tog*; rep from * to * 2 more times, work in seed st until last 3 sts, ssp, p1—8 sts dec, keeping the seed st patt uniform throughout—112 (112, 120, 128, 136) sts rem.

Note *With 2 sts decreased right next to each other each time, there should be no problem keeping the seed st even. The patt from the RS looks better with too many purl sts showing rather than too many knit sts; therefore, when in doubt on the WS knit the extra sts in order to stay in the seed stitch pattern and purl when in doubt on the RS.*

Next row (WS): Work seed st as est.

Work 6 more dec rows as above when piece measures:

9 (9, 10, 11, 12)" (22.8 [22.8, 25.5, 27.9, 30.4]cm)

12 (13, 14, 15, 16)" (30.4 [33, 35.6, 38.1, 40.6]cm)

16 (17, 18, 19, 20)" (40.6 [43.2, 45.7, 48.3, 50.8]cm)

19 (20, 21, 22, 23)" (48.3 [50.8, 53.3, 55.9, 58.4]cm)

22 (23, 24, 25, 26)" (55.9 [58.4, 61, 63.5, 66]cm)

25 (26, 27, 28, 29)" (63.5 [66, 68.6, 71.1, 73.7]cm)

When piece measures 27 (28, 29, 30, 31)" (68.6 [71.1, 73.7, 76.2, 78.7]cm) work 1 more dec row, omitting dec at the beg and end of the row *for sizes XS and S only*—58 (58, 64, 72, 80) sts rem after all dec rows have been worked.

When the skirt back is desired length, end after working a RS row.

Waistband

Next row (turning ridge, WS): Knit.

Work 1" (2.5cm) in St st (knit RS rows, purl WS rows). BO loosely.

Front

Cast on 142 (142, 150, 162, 170) sts with US size 5 (6, 6, 6, 6) needles, using long-tail cast on.

Work in seed st for 3 rows. Change to US size 7 (8, 8, 8, 8) needles.

Set Up Patterns

Row 1 (RS): P1, [k1, p1] 4 (4, 4, 5, 5) times, pm, work row 1 of Single Honeycomb over next 12 sts, pm [k1, p1] 4 (4, 4, 5, 5) times, pm, work row 1 of Claw Stitch over next 12 sts, pm, [k1, p1] 4 (4, 4, 5, 5) times, pm, work row 1 of Large Cable Patt over the next 44 (44, 52, 52, 60) sts, pm, [k1, p1] 4 (4, 4, 5, 5) times, pm, work row 1 of Claw Stitch over next 12 sts, pm [k1, cp1] 4 (4, 4, 5, 5) times, pm, work row 1 of Single Honeycomb over next 12 sts, pm, [k1, p1] 4 (4, 4, 5, 5) times, k1.

Continue in patts as est, slipping markers when you come to them and working seed st between cable panels, until piece measures 6 (7, 7, 7, 8)" (15.2 [17.8, 17.8, 17.8, 20.3] cm), ending after working a WS row.

Front Decrease Rows

Note *The front decreases are worked only in the seed st panels until there are 2 seed sts left in each panel (plus the 2 reverse St sts on either side) except the end panels, where there will be 5 seed sts plus 2 rev St sts on each side of the seed st panels.*

First Dec Row (RS): p1, p2tog, *work seed st until 2 sts before end of seed st panel, ssp; continue in large cable patt until next seed st panel, p2tog, rep from * across row, end on last seed st panel, ssp, p1. On following rows in each seed st panel, work in seed st, adjusting sts to follow seed st patt—130 (130, 138, 150, 158) sts rem.

Second Dec Row (RS): Repeat first dec row after skirt measures 12 (13, 14, 14, 14)" (30.5 [33, 35.6, 35.6, 35.6] cm)—118 (118, 126, 138, 146) sts rem.

Aran Long Skirt

Flat width:11½ (12½, 13½, 15, 16½)"
(29.2 [31.8, 34.3, 38.1, 42]cm)

Circumference: 23 (25, 27, 30, 33)"
(59 [64, 69, 76, 84]cm)

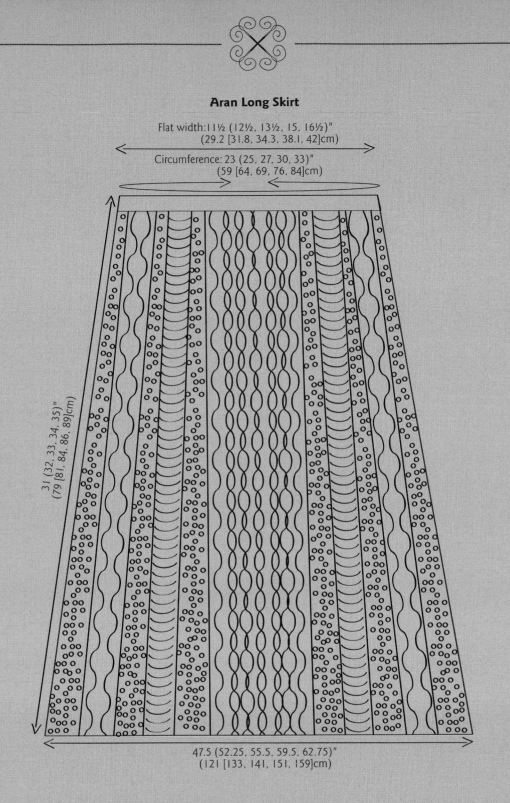

31 (32, 33, 34, 35)"
(79 [81, 84, 86, 89]cm)

47.5 (52.25, 55.5, 59.5, 62.75)"
(121 [133, 141, 151, 159]cm)

Third Dec Row (RS): When skirt measures 18 (19, 20, 18, 20)" (45.7 [48.3, 50.8, 45.7, 50.8]cm) dec, removing markers across row, by working p1, *p2tog, seed st 0 (0, 0, 2, 2), ssp, continue in cable patt until next seed st panel, rep from * across row, end on last seed st panel, p2tog, seed st 0 (0, 0, 2, 2), ssp, p1—106 (106, 114, 126, 134) sts rem.

From this point on, the reverse St sts on either side of the seed st panels will be included in the seed st panels. On the WS rows for sizes XS, S, and M, the sts will all be worked as knit, where previously, there were seed st panels.

Fourth Dec Row (RS): When skirt measures 23 (24, 25, 24, 25)" (58.4 [61, 63.5, 61, 63.5]cm) dec as follows: p1, p2tog, [also work ssp for size L and XL], p2 (the rev st sts), *work in pat across cable sts, p1, p2tog, seed st 0 (0, 0, 2, 2), ssp, p1, rep from * across row through last cable sts, p2, [p2tog for size L and XL], ssp, p1—96 (96, 104, 114, 122) sts rem.

Fifth Dec Row (RS): When skirt measures 28 (29, 30, 28, 29)" (71.1 [73.7, 76.2, 71.1, 73.7]cm), dec across row as follows: p1, p2tog, p1 (1, 1, 2, 2), *work next cable sts, p0 (0, 0, 1, 1) p2tog, ssp, p0, (0, 0, 1, 1), rep from * across row through last cable sts, p1 (1, 1, 2, 2), p2tog, p1—86 (86, 94, 104, 112) sts rem.

From this point on the WS rows for sizes L and XL will be worked all knit where the seed st panels were previously.

Sixth Dec Row (RS, size L and XL only): When skirt measures 31 (32)" (78.7 [81.3]cm) dec as follows: p1, p2tog, p1, *work cable sts, p2tog, ssp, rep from * across row through last cable sts, p1, p2tog, p1—86 (86, 94, 94, 102) sts rem.

Continue in patts as est until piece measures same as Back, ending after working row 21 (first choice), row 5, or row 13 of the large cable patt chart.

Change to US size 5 (6, 6, 6, 6) needles.

Waistband

Next row (turning ridge WS): Knit, dec across row by working k2tog each time you come to the previous seed st panels, now shown as 2 knit sts on the WS. When you come to the large cable sections in the middle of the row that show 4 knit sts on the WS (if you have ended after row 21, 5, or 13), k2tog twice. For size M only also decrease in the middle of the 4 small cable sections (shown as 8 purl sts on WS row) by working k3, k2tog, k3 in each of those 4 sections—70 (70, 72, 76, 82) sts rem.

Work 1" (2.5cm) in St st.

Bind off loosely.

Finishing

Sew side seams. Fold along turning ridge for waistband and attach waistband to the inside, leaving 2" (5cm) open for inserting elastic. Cut elastic to measure 1" (2.5cm) longer than waistline. Attach safety pin to one end of elastic and insert elastic into opening and work through, using the safety pin as a guide. With sewing needle and thread, sew ends of elastic together. Finish waistband seam.

Lightly block seams as necessary. It may also be necessary to stretch the seed stitch panels at the bottom of the front, as they are apt to draw up.

Designer Bio

Shirley MacNulty has been knitting for about 65 years, starting as a young child. She is a knitwear designer, tech editor, teacher, and author. Shirley is a charter member of AKD and TKGA and is a member of TNNA, and the Blue Ridge Fiber Guild. She divides her time between Wilmington, North Carolina, and Sugar Mountain, North Carolina, and has edited *Knitting News*, a subscription knitting newsletter for 20 years and owns Bay Country Boutique, a small knitting and gift shop.

Andean Plying

Some spinning and knitting skills are easily learned when sitting next to a friend at a festival, spin-in, or guild meeting. Hands-on learning is an important feature of most fiber arts events. Yet, some of us lack those communities and must learn from books or online. Here, my friend Nancy Shroyer, a well-known teacher on the festival circuit, takes the time to explain one of those tricky spinning skills.

Written by Nancy Shroyer

There's a legend that when the shepherds in the Andes Mountains of South America spun their yarn, they used a method of wrapping the yarn on their hand to ply the yarn on their spindles. This method of plying small amounts of singles is now known as Andean Plying. (A single is one strand of yarn; most yarns are then plied to create a stronger, thicker, more evenly balanced yarn.)

Here is how this process works:

1. Wrap a small amount of singles yarn around the thumb of your back spinning hand to anchor it.

2. Wind the yarn around the middle finger, back to the thumb, around the back of the hand to the little finger side, around the middle finger, around the back of the hand to the thumb side, then around the middle finger again.

3. Repeat the process is repeated until all the yarn is wound onto your hand.

4. Ease the yarn off the middle finger and allow it to slide down onto your wrist, forming a bracelet.

5. Remove the end wound around your anchoring thumb, and hold it with the wrapping end of the yarn. Splice these two yarns to the leader to ply onto the spindle.

Andean plying is a wonderful way to ply the yarn from one spindle or from a small amount of a single yarn on a spinning wheel bobbin. I use this method to make sample skeins for the same reason I make a swatch for knitting—to see if the results are what I had planned. I spin for about 10 minutes, wind the yarn in the Andean method, ply the yarn and finish it. Only after I knit with my sample yarn will I know if it's what I want for the

particular project. It's better to make the changes before spinning a pound of fiber with incorrect characteristics. Andean plying is also handy during a workshop where lots of sample skeins are spun and plied. It's much faster to ply from one bobbin than to have to spin onto two bobbins and then ply onto a third, having to stop and change bobbins in the process. After spinning and plying multiple bobbins, I always have some yarn left on the last bobbin that I can Andean ply rather than waste.

This method's advantage is that it doesn't require any additional tools. It's portable, as hands are always available. The disadvantage is that it works best with small amounts of yarn. If the spinner puts too much yarn onto her hand, it may become tangled while plying. If she winds too tightly, she risks numb and blue fingers. Also, if the doorbell rings or the baby cries, she's attached to her spinning. This wasn't much of a problem for the Andean shepherds, but for today's spinner with all our modern interruptions, dragging a wheel around with our spinning attached to our hands can be a problem.

An Andean plying tool takes the stress off the hands, allowing the spinner to stop in the middle of the process and come back to it. My company, Nancy's Knit Knacks, developed the Handy Andy to make Andean plying method easier and more convenient than the traditional hand method. The tool is shaped to fit in the hand, with a comfortable handle. It incorporates a peg at the top on which you can wrap the yarn and alleviate finger stress. The yarn is wrapped around the peg in a similar manner as on the hand, but if there's an interruption during the process, the spinner can simply put the tool onto the base and leave it. After the yarn wrapping is completed and the peg is removed, the yarn bracelet falls down onto the handle. The yarn is then plied back onto the spinning wheel (or drop spindle) while holding the tool, or the tool is placed in the base. The spinner can then ply in the same manner as using a lazy kate, leaving both hands free to tension and control the yarn.

To use the Handy Andy, follow these instructions:

1. Anchor your yarn end in the notch at the bottom of the handle (see photo on previous page).

2. Holding the handle in one hand and using the other hand, bring the yarn up the right side of the handle, wrap it around the peg clockwise, back to the right side of the handle, around the back of the handle to the front left side, around the peg counter clockwise,

and back to the left side of the handle, around the back of the handle to the right side.

3. Repeat the process until all the yarn is wrapped. It's important to always follow the same path.

4. When all the yarn is used, take the beginning yarn out of the notch and tie it to the end.

5. Before the peg is removed make sure the handle is being held, or the handle is in the base because the bracelet will drop. If it falls off the tool it will be difficult to maintain its shape. Once the bracelet is released, begin plying either by holding the handle, or parking it in the base.

The tool is successful with most yarns, but silk can be tricky. It can stick to itself and become difficult to control. Try letting silk rest longer on the bobbin or spindle and keep hold of the tool for better control.

Andean plying is a great way to use up leftover singles, or to make sample skeins with either the traditional hand method or the Handy Andy.

Writer Bio

Nancy Shroyer and her husband, Bob, own Nancy's Knit Knacks, a business that offers over 60 innovative products for spinning and weaving. Nancy teaches knitting and spinning classes at festivals, guilds, and yarn shops nationwide. To see more about the Handy Andy or learn more about Nancy's business, see www.nancysknitknacks.com.

Techniques

Although *Fiber Gatherings* is not a learn-to-knit book, I want to provide enough information so that beginning to intermediate crafters can successfully make all of the projects. This section includes instructions for special techniques used by the knit and crochet designers whose works are featured in this book. If you need instruction on basic knitting or crochet techniques, check out the many fine learn-to-knit books on the market, do an Internet search, or support your local yarn store by asking the friendly staff about their classes.

Knitting

The following knitting techniques are used in projects in this book. If a technique is used in only one project, it is included with the pattern.

Casting On

In most knitting projects, you can use whatever cast-on technique you prefer. In a few cases, the designers have suggested a specific technique to achieve special results.

Backwards loop cast-on (also called single cast-on)

1. Start with a slip knot or with a previously established piece of knitting. Wrap the working yarn around your thumb, back to front.

2. Pull working yarn to the back, holding it with your fingers, creating a cross in the yarn between your thumb and fingers.

3. Put needle tip in the loop alongside your thumb. Take your thumb out of the loop and pull on the working yarn to tighten your stitch on the needle.

Long tail cast-on (also called double cast-on)

1. Pull out a "long tail" of yarn about 1" (2.5cm) long for each stitch you need to cast on. Make a slip knot and put it on the needle. This is the first stitch.

2. With the tail of the yarn over your left thumb and the yarn attached to the ball over your index finger, pull the strands open. Grasp the strands in your palm, and pull the needle down to form a "V" between your thumb and index finger.

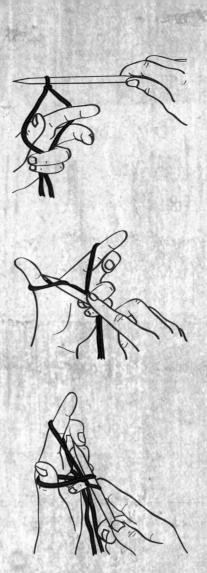

3. *Insert the needle into the loop on your thumb, from bottom to top. Bring the needle around the yarn on your index finger from right to left and catch the yarn on the needle. Then pull the yarn back through the loop on your thumb from top to bottom.

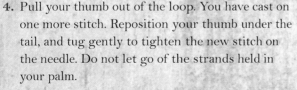

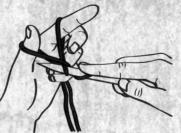

4. Pull your thumb out of the loop. You have cast on one more stitch. Reposition your thumb under the tail, and tug gently to tighten the new stitch on the needle. Do not let go of the strands held in your palm.

5. Repeat from * until you have the desired number of stitches.

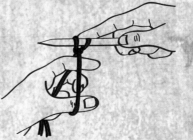

Special Knitting Techniques
Tips for Knitting with Two Circular Needles

When knitting in the round, a circular needle must be shorter than the circumference of the knitting so the stitches reach around the needle. When a knitted piece, like a sock, mitten, or sleeve cuff is too small to fit on a circular needle, I use double-pointed needles. Some knitters prefer to work on two circular needles, and the Festive Fingerless Mitts pattern on page 24 uses this technique. Whether you choose to use double-pointed needles or two circular needles, your end result will look the same. Here are the basics for using two circular needles:

1. Divide your stitches evenly onto two circular needles so the first needle holds the first half of the round and the second needle holds the second half of the round.

2. To knit a round, use the first needle only and knit the first half of the round. Then turn the work around so the second half of the round faces you, and switch to the second needle only to knit the second half of the round. The stitches always stay on the same needle. You may find it helpful to use needles that are different colors to help keep track.

Sewing Seams

Just as with casting on or binding off, in most knitting patterns you can sew seams using your favorite technique. In a few cases, designers recommend a specific technique for best results on their projects.

Running stitch

A running stitch can be used for small seams or for basting pieces together to test the fit. Simply run a tapestry needle with matching yarn up and down through the two pieces of fabric at regular intervals.

Overcast stitch (also called whip stitch)

1. With the right sides of the fabric facing up, place the two pieces to be seamed on a flat surface.

2. *With a tapestry needle and matching yarn, use one smooth motion to catch the stitch on the edge of one piece of knitting and then catch a stitch on the other piece. Repeat from * until entire seam is stitched.

Whipstitch

Mattress stitch (also sometimes called weaving)

1. With the right sides facing up, place the two pieces to be seamed on a flat surface.

2. *With a tapestry needle and matching yarn, go under the bar between first and second stitches near the edge of one piece of knitting, then repeat on the other piece.

3. Repeat from * until entire seam is stitched, pulling gently to tighten seam after every few stitches.

Three-needle bind-off

1. Place the two pieces on knitting needles so the right sides of each piece are facing each other with the needles parallel. *Both pieces should have the exact same number of stitches.*

2. *Insert a third needle one size larger through the leading edge of the first stitch on each needle. Knit these stitches together as one, leaving 1 st on the right-hand needle.

3. Repeat from *, slipping the older stitch on the left-hand needle over newer stitch to bind off.

Blocking

For best results, knitted and crocheted pieces should be blocked after completion. There are several ways to block:

- For garment pieces, wet the pieces by soaking or spraying with water, form them to the dimensions specified in the pattern, and leave to dry. If desired, pin the pieces in shape until try.

- For ribbing or other stretchy pieces, wash the piece in tepid water and dry flat without stretching or pinning.

- For natural fibers, some prefer to use steaming as a blocking method. Using a hot iron, gently hold the steaming iron above the pinned-out garment piece. This provides a harder block but is slightly more dangerous than the above options. *Note: Man-made fibers will melt using this process.*

- For lace, soak the piece in tepid water until it is saturated, then stretch it to the dimensions specified in the pattern and pin it in place until dry. Blocking wires can also be use to stretch and block lace. They are available from knitting stores and online retailers, and usually come with instructions.

Knitting from Charts

All of the projects in this book that have charted patterns also provide the instructions in text. If you already know how to work from charts, you may find that they speed up your knitting and reduce errors. If you haven't knit from charts yet, you can try it on these projects, or follow the line-by-line instructions instead.

Charts are read from bottom to top, right to left for right side rows (odd rows, knit), and left to right for wrong side rows (even rows, purl). Each square represents one stitch.

Crochet

For knitters who are not familiar with crochet stitches, the following sections should give you enough of a foundation to get started.

Chain

To begin a crochet piece, you often create a chain of stitches to use as a foundation. Crochet can also be added directly to a piece of knitting.

1. Make a slipknot on your hook. *Bring the yarn over the hook from back to front.

2. Bring the yarn through the loop (lp) on your hook. Rep from * until chain is desired length.

Single Crochet

1. Working from right to left: *Insert the hook into the next stitch. Bring the yarn over the hook and pull the working yarn through the loop on the hook. You now have two loops on your hook.

2. Bring the yarn over the hook again and pull the yarn through both loops. One loop remains on the hook. Repeat from * for the desired number of stitches.

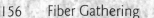

Crab Stitch (Reverse Single Crochet)

1. Working from *left to right*: *Insert the hook into the next stitch to the *right* of your hook. Bring the yarn over the hook and pull the yarn through the stitch.

2. Yarn over and pull the yarn through both loops. One loop remains on the hook. Repeat from * for the desired number of stitches.

Double Crochet

1. Working from right to left: *Bring the yarn over the hook and insert the hook into the next stitch; bring the yarn over the hook and pull the yarn through the stitch. Three loops are on the hook.

2. Yarn over and pull the yarn through the first two loops on the hook; two loops remain on the hook.

3. Yarn over and pull the yarn through the last two loops on the hook; one loop remains on the hook. Repeat from * for the desired number of stitches.

Slip Stitch

This stitch is used to join rounds of crochet and to work short areas without adding length to the piece.

1. Working from right to left: *Insert the hook into the next stitch.
2. Bring the yarn over the hook, and pull the hook through the stitch and the loop on your hook.
3. Repeat from * until the desired number of slip stitches have been worked.

Fastening off

Since you only have one crochet stitch on the hook at a time, there is no need to bind off in crochet. To fasten off your work, cut the working yarn, pull the end through the last loop, and tug gently to tighten.

Table of Abbreviations

This table includes the basic knitting and crochet abbreviations used in this book. Some special abbreviations are defined within the patterns.

( )	repeat the instructions in the brackets the specified number of times		pf&b	purl into the front and back of the same stitch (increase)
*	repeat the instructions after the * as instructed		pm	place marker
bl	back loop (crochet)		pw	purlwise
CC	contrasting color		rem	remain
ch	chain(s)		rep	repeat
cm	centimeter(s)		rev sc	reverse single crochet (crab stitch)
dc	double crochet(s)		rnd(s)	round(s)
dec	decrease(s); decreasing		RS	right side
dpn(s)	double pointed needle(s)		sc	single crochet(s)
est	establish(ed)		sl	slip (knit)
fl	front loop (crochet)		sl st	slip stitch (crochet)
g	gram		sl1, k1, psso	slip 1, knit 1, pass slipped stitch over
inc	increase(s); increasing		sl1, k2tog, psso	slip 1 kw, k2tog, pass slipped stitch over
K or k	knit		sm	slip marker
k2tog	knit 2 together		ssk	slip, slip, knit
kf&b	knit into the front and back of the same stitch (increase)		St st	Stockinette stitch; Stocking stitch
kw	knitwise		st(s)	Stitch(es)
MC	main color		WS	wrong side
oz	ounce(s)		wyib	with yarn in back
P or p	purl		wyif	with yarn in front
p2tog	purl 2 together		yd	yard(s)
patt	pattern		YO	yarn over

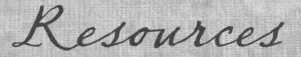

Resources

Below is the contact information for the yarns, tools and accessories used in *Fiber Gathering's* project models. In some cases, this is the name of a small farm business, in others, a large wholesale yarn distributor. Please be aware that businesses and yarn lines change over time, so feel free to substitute yarns or tools from your local yarn shop or fiber festival if the exact yarns used in the models are no longer available.

Yarns, Tools and Accessories

The Barefoot Spinner
HC79, Box 31-A
Romney, WV 26757
(304) 822-5767
twpritch@access.mountain.net

Blue Sky Alpacas, Inc
PO Box 88
Cedar, MN 55011
(888) 460-8862
info@blueskyalpacas.com
www.blueskyalpacas.com

Brooks Farm
412 Old Red Oak Rd.
Lancaster, TX 75146
(972) 227-1593
info@brooksfarmyarn.com
www.brooksfarmyarn.com

Brown Sheep Company, Inc.
100662 County Road 16
Mitchell, NE 69357
(800) 826-9136
Fax (308) 635-2143
www.brownsheep.com

Cascade Yarns
1224 Andover Park East
P.O. Box 58168
Tukwila, WA 58168
(800) 548-1048
www.cascadeyarns.com

Decadent Fibers
 (owned by two partners)
7 Cortland Drive
Kinderhook, NY 12106
(518) 265-9142

Decadent Fibers
 (owned by two partners)
708 Bridge Street
Selkirk, NY 12158
(518) 767-9430
Fax: (518) 758-8671
thedecadents@decadentfibers.
 com
www.decadentfibers.com

Green Mountain Spinnery
Box 568
Putney, VT 05346
(802) 387-4528
Fax: (802) 387-4841
spinnery@sover.net
www.spinnery.com

Honey Lane Farms
289 Honey Lane
Friday Harbor, WA 98250
(360) 378-1895
www.honeylanefarms.com

Hooked on Ewe
5339 S. State Road
Ionia, MI 48846
(616) 527-1079
www.harwoodhookedonewe.
 com

Knit Picks
13118 N.E. 4th St.,
Vancouver, WA 98684
(800) 574-1323
 www.knitpicks.com

La Lana Wools
136 C Paseo del Pueblo Norte
Taos, NM 87571
(505) 758-9631
(888) 377-9631
lalana@lalanawools.com
www.lalanawools.com

Lorna's Laces
4229 North Honore Street
Chicago, IL 60613
(773) 935-3803
Fax: (773) 935-3804
yarn@lornaslaces.net
www.lornaslaces.net

Moda Dea
Coats Moda Dea
P.O. Box 12229
Greenville, SC
29612-0229
(800) 648-1479
www.modadea.com

Nancy's Knit Knacks
104 Hobblebrook Ct.
Cary, NC 27518
(800) 731-5648
Fax: (919) 387-3666
www.nancysknitknacks.com

Spirit Trails Fiberworks
P.O. Box 197
Sperryville, VA 22740-0197
(703) 309-3199
info@spirit-trail.net
www.spirit-trail.net

Tongue River Farm Yarns
c/o Bloomin' Acres Farm
16088 Hwy 59 South
Lincoln, AR 72744-9289
(479) 848-3060
bloominacres@pgtc.com
www.bloominacresfarm.com

The Pin featured in the Fish
Tail Vest is available from:

Designs by Romi
Rosemary Hill
73 Bosworth Lane
Geyserville, CA 95441
(707) 857-3399
romi@designsbyromi.com
www.designsbyromi.com

Spinning and Fiber Supplies

Spinning Supplies are available at many stores and farms nationwide. There are many names of fiber producers and suppliers throughout the book as well. Here are a few shops that are often at festivals and also have online stores. If you're looking specifically for raw wool, it's easiest to shop in person at a festival, farm or store. Look locally first!

Susan's Fiber Shop
N250 Hwy A
Columbus, WI 53925
(920) 623-4237
susan@susansfibershop.com
www.susansfibershop.com

**Carol Leigh's Hillcreek
    Fiber Studio**
7001 S Hill Creek Rd
Columbia, MO 65203
(800) TRI-WEAV (874-9328)
Service_Support@
    HillcreekFiberStudio.com
www.hillcreekfiberstudio.
    com

Fiber Festival Web Sites

Most festivals have their own Web pages. Here are the Web pages for the public events and activities listed in the order they appear in the book:

**Maryland Sheep and
    Wool Festival**
www.sheepandwool.org

**New York State Sheep and
    Wool Festival**
www.sheepandwool.com

**New Hampshire Sheep and
    Wool Festival**
www.nhswga.com/content/
    view/36/33

**Southeastern Animal
    Fiber Fair**
www.saffsite.org

**The Tennessee State Fair:
    Spinning Competition
    and Fleece Auction**
www.tennesseestatefair.org

Michigan Fiber Festival
www.michiganfiberfestival.
    info

**Heart of America Sheep
    Show and Fiber Fest**
www.moncwga.com

Black Sheep Gathering
www.blacksheepgathering.
    org

Estes Park Wool Market
www.estesnet.com/Events/
    woolmarket.htm

The Wool Festival at Taos
www.taoswoolfestival.org

**Knitting Guild of
    Greater Buffalo**
www.buffaloknittingguild.
    org/membership.html

There's no conclusive listing to all festivals everywhere, but Knitters Review does a great job of summarizing most of the North American events:

www.knittersreview.com/
    upcoming_events.asp

Index